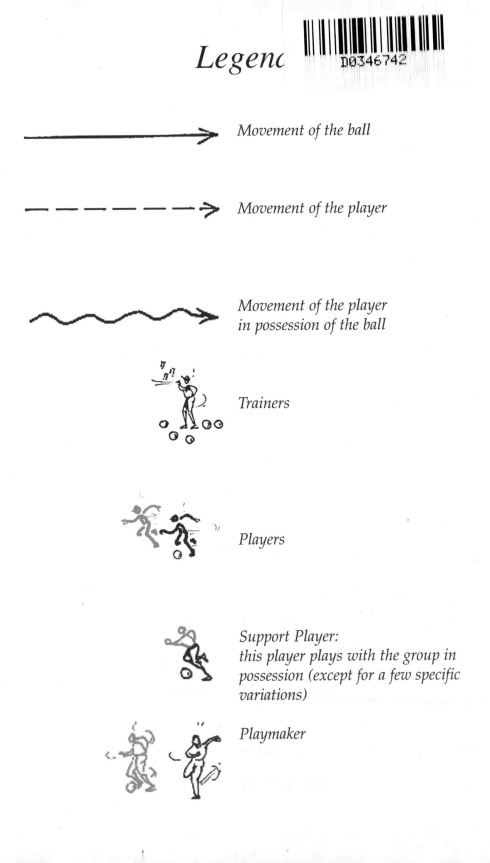

Movement of the ball

Movement of the player

Movement of the player
in possession of the ball

Trainers

Players

Support Player:
this player plays with the group in
possession (except for a few specific
variations)

Playmaker

Introduction

Fast play is constructed during training

A team game like soccer needs skillful players who can keep going at a face pace while showing precision, skill and creativity.

We know that we are not talking to coaches who think that every athlete's quality is owed to his natural ability or that games are won through luck and improvised moves on the playing field but even so we feel it is essential to stress our conviction that the speed of play greatly depends on the individual players' mental training for fast play.

This is a habit that one isn't born with or that comes forth when needed during the game. It is the result of continuous training where the activity is constantly directed at the development of fast moves. During play the player must receive motor stimuli not only of a certain quantity but also of a certain quality so that he can refine his perception of the game. Correct perception will supply the athlete with a series of motor abilities which will be useful in speeding up the player's game. The perception of a move or of a series of moves does not stand alone, it is the basis for the understanding of the team action. The player goes beyond the simple understanding of the move in front of him to capture the essential data necessary for motor activity.

The combination of experiences and perception forms an athlete who becomes an expert and who doesn't only know how to memorize certain phases of the game so as to automatize the necessary movements but who also knows how to associate the different combinations to create new solutions to play.

If the athlete perfects his motor ability he will know how to direct these abilities to new situations.

Whatever the athlete recognizes in training he will be able to use to predict the play and be able to prepare himself for sudden motor situations with an adequate response. It is indispensable for the athlete to be able to evaluate time and space if he is to understand the rhythm of play and elaborate a fast tactical response both from a mental and physical point of view.

The capability of providing a correct reaction to the stimuli received during play depends greatly on the preparation done during training. This explains the need to put players in situations which they will surely come up against in the regular game, the mechanism of mental transfer will facilitate situations in play.

Motor ability will allow for a minor consumption of psychological energy also when confronted with more complex situations. The athlete will have automatized certain necessary movements so that he can channel his psychic concentration and his physical ability to resolve motor combinations where creativity in concrete situations is necessary.

Tactical Build-Up in the Attacking Game

One of the most complex and significant aspects of the game of soccer is the build-up of the attack. It is in the attacking game that the player's ability to react correctly to complex situations comes to the fore.

The team attacking game is, in fact, a process of construction which starts with the individual and implies a profound analysis of the stronger qualities and weaker points of each player.

For a long time the attention paid to the winning tactical strategies in the game of soccer were such that the psycho-physical preparation and technique of the individual player were neglected.

A team must have quality athletes who are capable of using their individual technical abilities in different positions, quick to understand a defense, able to penetrate the same defense, and single out their area of play.

The actual game teaches us that every playing situation is different from the one that preceded it. Because of this, fast reactions are essential. These are reactions which haven't been studied on the drawing board but require the perception of the opponent's move.

One of the most important factors in a successful attack is its flexibility. This allows a constructive adaptation to various situations of play. It is important to be able to make use of alternative choices other than the moves worked out before the game. This is the fundamental principle for effective action. The team must, therefore, be trained with exercises that oblige the players to make exact evaluations in critical moments and look for suitable solutions without having to refer to a prearranged strategy that is ineffective in the given situation.

The athlete who considers himself part of a system will be able to examine the game as a whole, from a rational point of view. He will be able to analyze the various situations without simply sticking to his role.

Nowadays only a highly organized team can control the various types of pressure applied. That is why when certain basic principles are respected by the individual players the whole team will benefit tactically. They must be learned before the tactical moves in order to allow the game to open up over the entire pitch.

The attacking players trained according to these principles must:

1. be able to work in defense using various zones of defense, marking etc. They must learn this in order to be able to understand the moves of their defending opponents. This helps the attacking players to understand what type of attacking move will be conceded by the defense and who is best suited to carrying out the move. It is important to remember that in whatever position he may be, the attacking player in possession of the ball immediately becomes a defender when his opponent wins possession;

2. play with freedom of movement inside a flexible, organized attacking system;

3. train with the idea that the opponent knows their game perfectly. In this way the psychological barrier is broken;

4. beat the opponent's defense before it moves into counterattack on every ball won. During training it is advisable to get used to winning the ball from a bad pass and opening up the play;

5. discourage the opponent from marking tightly. Try to penetrate the defense with a suitable move without losing possession. If the attack is forced to organize an offensive "strategy" in midfield it means that the pressure has already given the advantage to the opponent;

6. know how to take advantage of the free spaces for passes, to make the attack flexible and make the players realize that set tactics are not always easy to use during play.

A correct preparation for attacking play cannot exclude the player's ability to analyze the various possibilities available to him in play, he must consider that the logic of every move is composed of three levels:

1. collective movement which brings into play the mutual and opposite reactions of both opponents;

2. movement in each zone (made up of three or four players);

3. individual action.

In the mind of the well-trained player none of these phases cän exist without the other and during play the mental configuration will translate into practice and the player will fit into the move from the point of view of timing and space.

An effective attacking game that creates possibilities against the standard contemporary defensive formations is one which is based on movement. It implies continuous movement from the players within a set game plan. This attacking formation must be capable of taking advantage of the weak points of the opponents' defense. The well-trained player will act according to the following principles.

A. continuous movement: the attack moves forward with an abundance of players that moves from one side of the pitch to the other to create openings which are well defined, open spaces in the defense to tire the defense and keep it in constant movement;

B. penetrating attack: use the central corridor in attack to leave the attacking players on the wings unmarked to allow surprise shots on goal. During this phase the players are obliged to make rapid decisions so as not to lose the ball and their confidence is built up in responsible positions;

C. changes of position: new moves are created when players can adapt to different positions. In this way openings are created followed by finishing chances. Such a training program will specialize the players and improve their control of the ball and their natural movement. During play the player will realize how to participate in the game from his own moves rather than from impersonal training strategies from the drawing board.

Soccer is a player's game. American football is, on the other hand, a coach's game. The instructor must, therefore, teach well during training but he must only be a guide in the game itself. The players must realize that in a given movement, they are in the best position to finish.

In this way they learn to read the defensive tactics and find the space for the finishing touch.

This confirms that for the construction of a valid attacking game attention must be paid to the individual capacities of the single player rather than to rigid tactical strategies. In this way the individual player will tackle the game with solutions that are ever more rational, effective and conclusive.

CHAPTER ONE

Perfection of the move

1) Maintaining possession.
2) Improve dribbling and 1-2 combinations

The exercises in this chapter are designed to perfect the technical ability of the player. The individual speed of the player is necessary to make the team game more effective thus guaranteeing greater fluidity and technical perfection.

The success of this aspect of the game depends on the combination of rhythm and execution: the criteria of repetition and adequate rhythm will determine the consolidation and development of motor qualities in skill co-ordination, articulation, speed and strength.

These motor skills improve and thus their application becomes easier over longer periods of time and also in their complexity.

Exercise n. 1

Players
8.

Duration
15'/20'.

Objectives
Long precise passes to perfect control of the ball and dribble free of the opponent.

Description
The players of the pair A-B stand at a distance of about 30/35 meters from one another. They play long precise passes to each other. The pair C-D try to intercept the passes. Once the opponents manage to get possession of the ball the roles are inverted. The exercise should be done at the same time by the pairs G-E and L-F.

Variations
1) Alternate between left and right foot when performing long passes.
2) At R's signal the pairs quickly exchange places.
3) At R's signal the pairs A-B and G-E exchange passes.

Example n. 2

Players
2 + 2 support players + 1 goalkeeper.

Duration
25/30 shots from both sides of the pitch. After 5 shots all players, including the two support players exchange positions.

Objectives
Creative technical co-ordination through flow of movement.

Description
The two support players cross balls in from the corners. Two players from group A volley the ball in from the edge of the penalty area. The exercise is to be repeated in the opposite corner with two other support players and group B.

Variations
1) The player from group A volleys the ball with his right foot while the one from group B uses his left foot.
2) The players from both groups alternate shots with left and right.

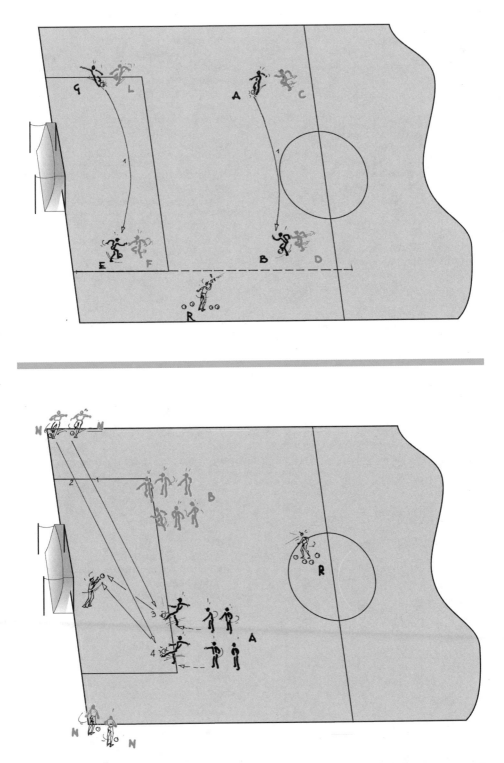

Exercise n. 3

Players
1 + 1 support player
+ 1 goalkeeper.

Duration
25/30 crosses from both corners with the support players changing position with the groups after every ten crosses.

Objectives
Flow of movement for co-ordinated precision of technique on shots.

Description
As B moves forward to the edge of the penalty area the support player delivers a cross from the corner. B strikes the ball on the volley with his left. The exercise is to be repeated in quick succession in the opposite corner with another support player who plays the ball for group A.

Variations
1) The player on the edge of the penalty area takes the cross with his left and shoots with his right.
2) From the support player's lob, B volleys the ball to A on the opposite side. A shoots on the volley.
3) B volleys the ball to the left of the goalkeeper while A sends the ball to the right.

Exercise n. 4

Players
1 + 1 support player
+ 1 goalkeeper

Duration
25/30 crosses from both corners.

Objectives
Flow of movement for co-ordinated precision of technique.

Description
The support player plays a long high cross, B plays an attacking header from the edge of the penalty area. The exercise is to be repeated from the other corner with the other support player playing the ball to A.

Variations
1) The two support players cross balls at the same time for their respective groups.
2) The support players cross balls in moderate succession for one of the players of the two groups.
3) First time volley from the edge of the penalty area.

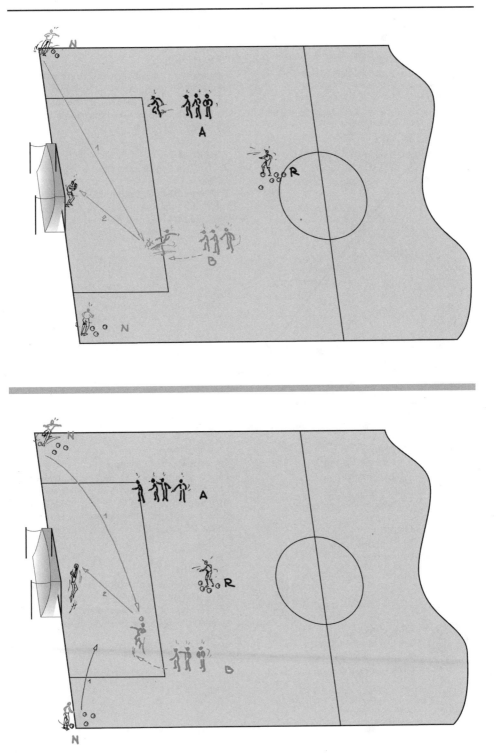

Exercise n. 5

Players
3 + 2 goalkeepers.

Duration
30/50 shots. Every 8/10 shots the players should exchange places.

Objectives
Control of the ball and timing of the concluding header.

Description
A starts with the ball. A and C make a run along the wings from the halfway line. They play long passes to each other. The third player, B, finishes the move with a header from C1's long high cross.

Variations
1) The two goalkeepers jump to head the ball before B.
2) A1 and B1 both jump to head the ball blocked by the goalkeepers.
3) A1 and C1 alternate the final cross to B.

Exercise n. 6

Players
6 + 1 support player + 1 goalkeeper.

Duration
25/30 crosses from both corners.

Objectives
Control of the ball and build-up of attack with passes along the wings.

Description
On a small pitch, the support player crosses balls to group 2A on the right wing. B attempts to intercept the crosses. With a series of 1-2's they move into area **1** to shoot diagonally at goal. The support player crosses to group 2C on the left wing. D attempts to intercept the crosses.

Variations
1) If the defender intercepts the ball he may move in from the wing to shoot at goal.
2) A second support player stands outside the area to receive a cross from A or C to head at goal.
3) 3 against 2 dribbling the ball.

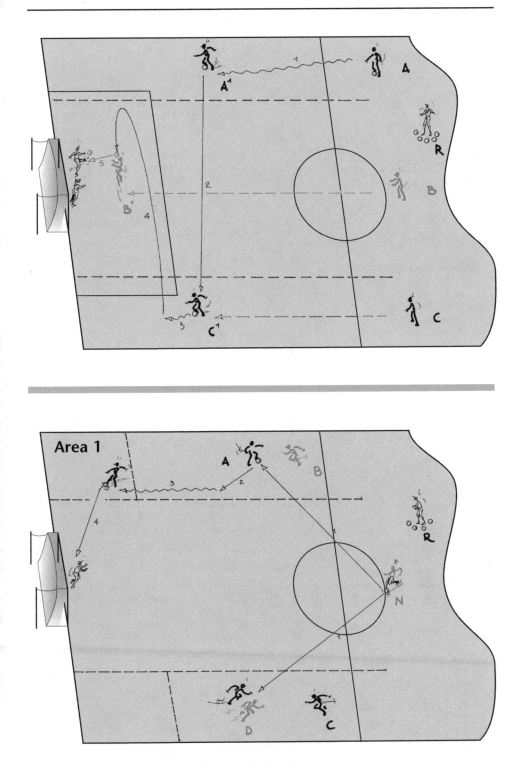

Area 1

Exercise n. 7

Players
2 + 1 support player
+ 1 goalkeeper.

Duration
25/30 shots. Every 5
shots the players
switch places.

Objectives
Perfection of co-ordina-
tion for reflex and
power on shot.

Description
The support player crosses the ball in from the
corner to A. A touches the ball on to B who
shoots at goal on the volley. The exercise is to
be carried out in the opposite corner with the
other support player, C and D.

Variations
1) Groups B and D head the ball towards the
net.
2) From the corner kick, A plays the ball to
group D and C plays the ball to group B.
3) A and C head the ball down to groups B and
D for first time shots.

Exercise n. 8

Players
2 + 4 goalkeepers.

Duration
30/40 alternating shots.
Every 5 shots the goal-
keepers switch with the
attacking players.

Objectives
Exercise for control and
timing of final header.

Description
A is in possession of the ball, with B he makes
a run along the wings from the halfway line.
From the edge of the box A floats a long high
ball in for B on the head. The keepers can only
use their feet to save. C and D repeat the exercise in the opposite direction.

Variations
1) One of the keepers comes out of the goal to
head the ball with B.
2) Two players jump together to play the shot.
One dummies the ball, the other shoots.
3) The keepers play the ball directly out to the
half-way line.

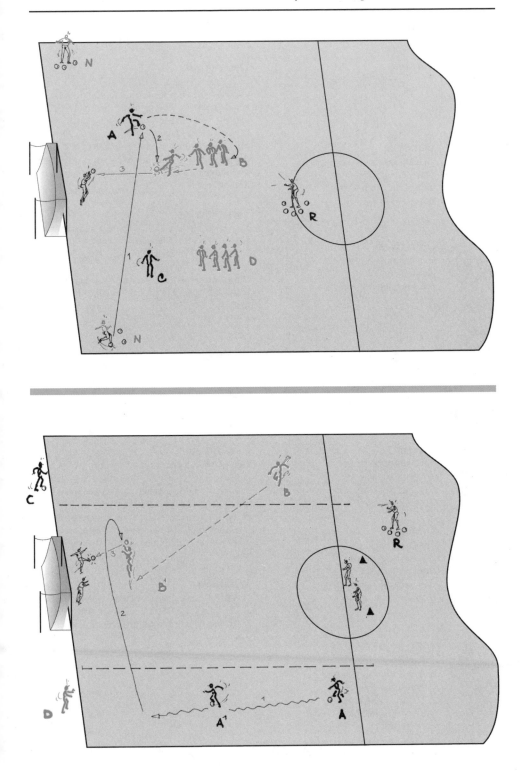

Exercise n. 9

Players
10 + 2 support players.

Duration
15 shots. Every 3 shots play changes from one half of the pitch to the other.

Objectives
Tactical move to keep possession and adapt players to change of play.

Description
In the play areas **1** and **2**, 3A and 2B and 3 B and 2A battle for possession to play into the small goals. In playing area **1** group 3A dribbles the ball to keep possession while 2B tries to open up the play to attack the goal. The roles are inverted in play area **2**. At R's signal the players pass the ball to the support player and move to the opposite playing area to continue the play.

Variations
1) In each playing area at R's signal a support player plays the ball from one area to the other.
2) 3 against 3 in each play area. Three touch play.
3) 4 against 4 in each playing area with two passing players per group who are not allowed to shoot.

Exercise n. 10

Players
2 + 2 support players + 1 goalkeeper.

Duration
The two attacking players make a run from centerfield and finish on the goal line in under 30 seconds.

Objectives
1. Rapid control of the ball and rapid finishing on first time shot.
2. The intervention of the two support players determines the finishing of the two players A and B.

Description
Two players A and B make a run from the halfway line. They play first touch diagonal balls to each other. When they get to the edge of the box they are tackled by the two support players who move in from the touchline to intercept them. The exercise continues with other players making runs from the halfway line.

Variations
1) A dribbles past support player and shoots.
2) The two support players tackle A together.
3) B's shot is blocked by the keeper.

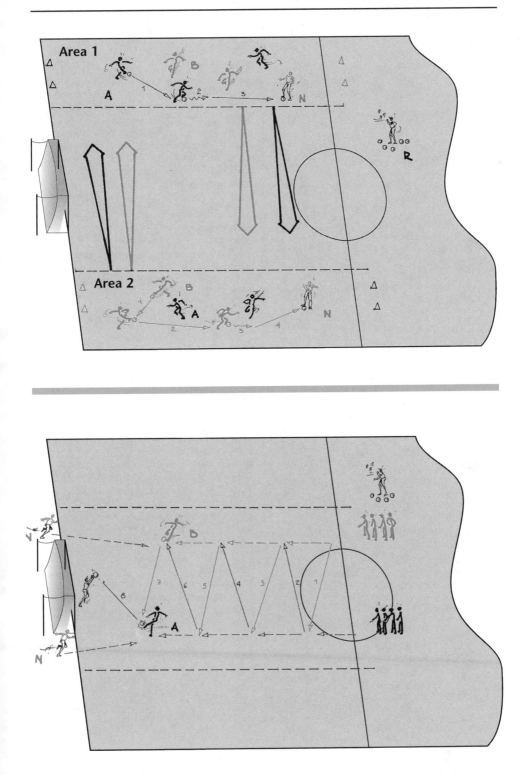

Exercise n. 11

Players
12.

Duration
15'/20'.

Objectives
Build-up of consistent movement of players and ball.

Description
3A and 3B play each other in the areas **1** and **2**. They dribble the ball and play 1-2 combinations. Group A plays fast passes to keep possession in area **1**. They are defended by two members of group B. The third B player can intercept the passing with his hands to throw to his team-mates in area **2**. If the designated player is not able to intercept the ball the changes from one field to another are decided by R.

Variations
1) Limit touches.
2) The designated player can only intercept the ball and play it with his feet.
3) The designated player can only intercept high balls.

Exercise n. 12

Players
6.

Duration
15'/20'.

Objectives
1. Exercise for possession.
2. Players adapt from attacking player to defender.

Description
In the areas of play on the flanks, A and B are defended by C and D and E are defended by F. They play 1-2's to keep possession. At R's signal the two groups exchange balls with long passes. If F and C manage to gain possession they join with another player to form a pair in the area to continue play.

Variations
1) In each area of play 4 play against 3.
2) Play with right and left feet.
3) Reduce touches as much as possible.

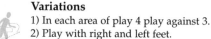

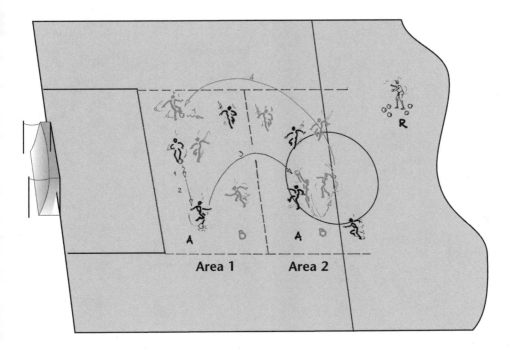

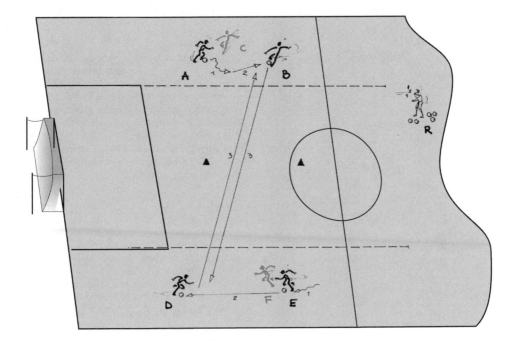

Exercise n. 13

Players
6 + 1 goalkeeper.

Duration
15/20 times.
Exchange places every two minutes.

Objectives
1. Move to introduce two players into play.
2. Perfection of finishing header.

Description
Group 3A attacks the goal defended by 2B and the keeper. R plays the ball to A who moves down the wing. He floats in a high ball for the head of one of his teammates. A third player from group B moves in from midfield when R plays the all to A. The attacking players are only to head the ball.

Variations
1) Exchange of positions after each header at goal.
2) One of the support players acts as play maker both in defense and in attack.

Exercise n. 14

Players
6 + 1 goalkeeper.

Duration
20'.

Objectives
Improve dribbling technique to pass opponent.

Description
Group 3A moves forward from the halfway line with two-touch play to attack the goal defended by the keeper and 2B. A player from group A moves in to take a long ball on the wing. At the same time another player moves in to back up the defense and attack the player in possession of the ball. The player in possession attempts to dribble past his opponents and pass to other members of his team.

Variations
1) Rapid exchange of places when group B gains possession.
2) At R's signal 4 support players move in from off the goal line. They are only to play one touch passes to each other.
3) At R's signal two attacking players move in from off the goal line to substitute two of the players from group A.

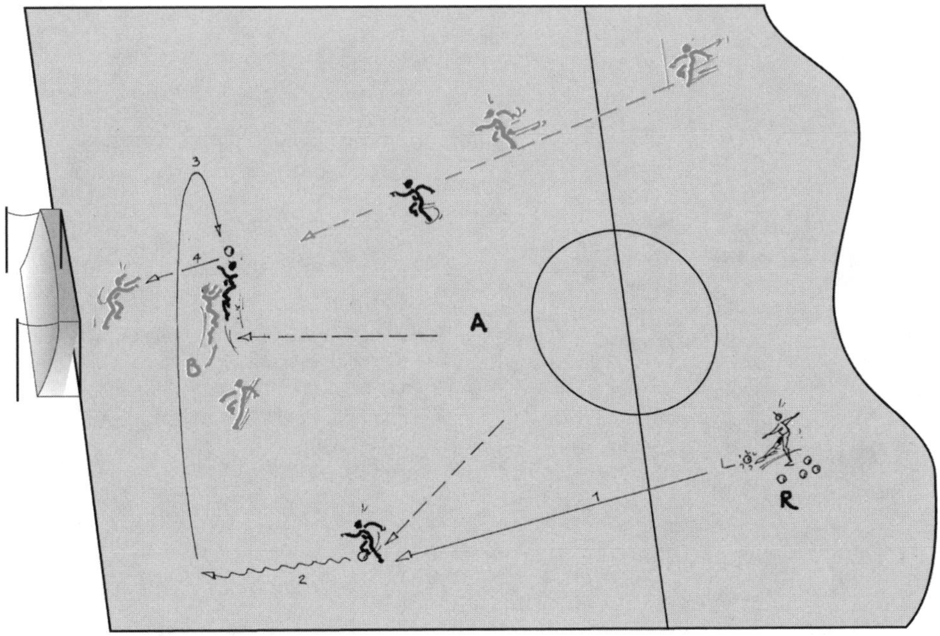
3
4
A
B
1
2
R

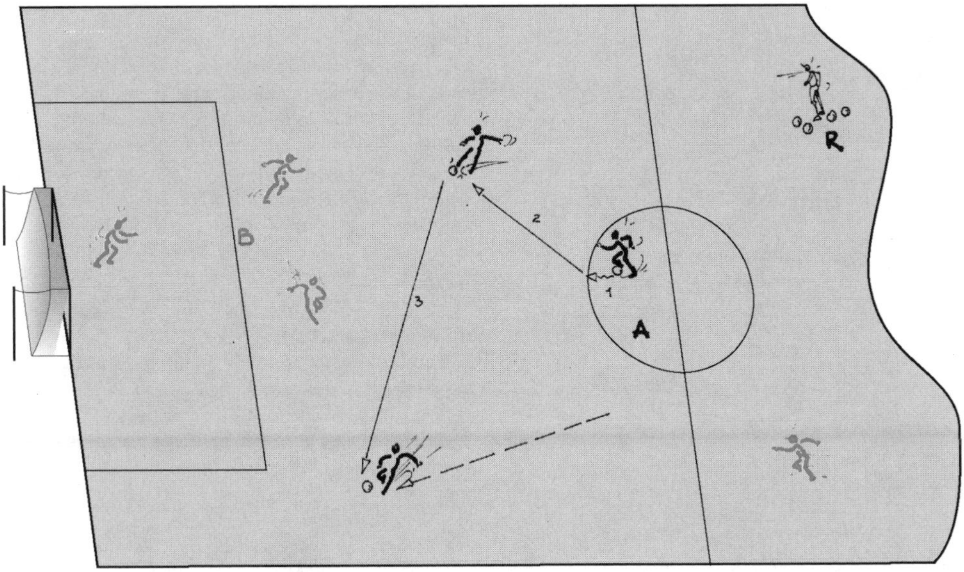
R
B
2
1
3
A

Exercise n. 15

Players
8.

Duration
15 minutes.

Objectives
Tactical moves for acceleration in play.

Description
In the areas of play marked **1** and **2**, group 2A plays against group 2B. At a signal from R one group concedes possession to the other and play continues. One player from each group has the task of using the pitch to build up moves and speed up play.

Variations
1) Change of play from one area of play to another with low lobs.
2) Pressure play to gain possession.
3) Alternate between use of left and right feet.

Exercise n. 16

Players
3.

Duration
15/20 minutes. Every three moves players exchange places.

Objectives
1) Tactical move for attacking player in possession of the ball.
2) Improvement of dribbling skills to pass opponent and finish.

Description
In a restricted area of the pitch A plays long balls of about 15/20 meters alternately to B and C. A alternates left and right foot when passing the ball. At a signal from R, A dribbles the ball towards the small 3 m. goal which is defended by B and C.

Variations
1) At R's signal another defender and support player move into play.
2) Exchange of pairs inside the area. At R's signal two players attack the big goal defended by a goalkeeper and two other players.
3) Dribbling and pressure play.
4) A exchanges places with B and C.

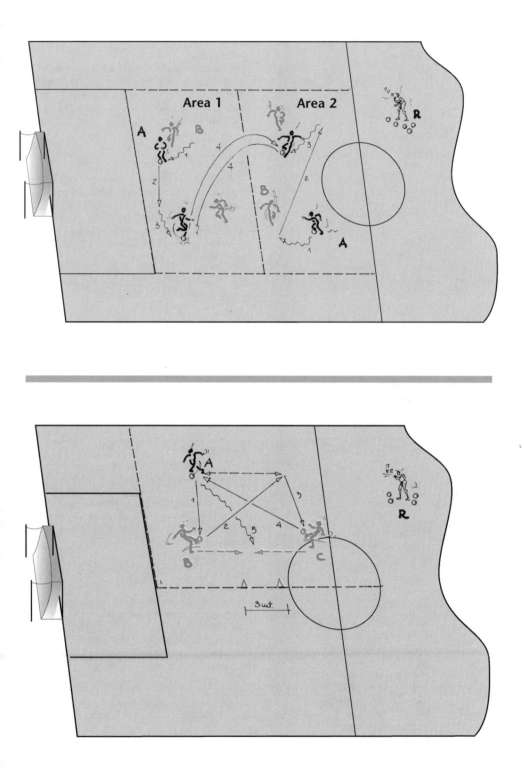

Exercise n. 17

Players
4.

Duration
10'/20'.

Objectives
Rapidity of player attacking goal.

Description
The pairs A-B and C-D pass the ball to each other. At R's signal, the player in possession of the ball attacks a 3-meter goal defended by a player from the other pair. A is defended by C and D is defended by B.

Variations
1) 2 against 2 instead of 1 against 1. Two players attack one goal and two others defend it.
2) Exchange between the pairs outside the area. At R's signal they play 2 against 2 with a single ball. The keeper defends the goal.
3) Switch positions between attacking players and defenders.

Exercise n. 18

Players
10.

Duration
Five 5 minute sessions.

Objectives
1) Tactical play for superior number of attacking players and for development of fast attacking moves.
2) The exercise must keep the two defenders in play. They must use as much of their own area as possible.

Description
Group 2A defends against group 3B in area **1**. Group 2B defends against group 3A in area **2**. The exercise involves the defending group of one area playing the ball to the attacking group in the opposite area. The attacking group plays three touch moves and take the ball over the defended 20-meter mark.

Variations
1) After every five minutes the roles must be switched between attacking players and defenders.
2) 7 against 5 in a bigger area with a keeper.
3) Alter amount of touches allowed
4) Cross the 20-meter mark dribbling the ball.

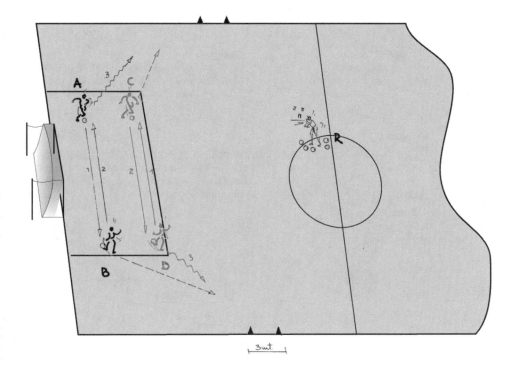

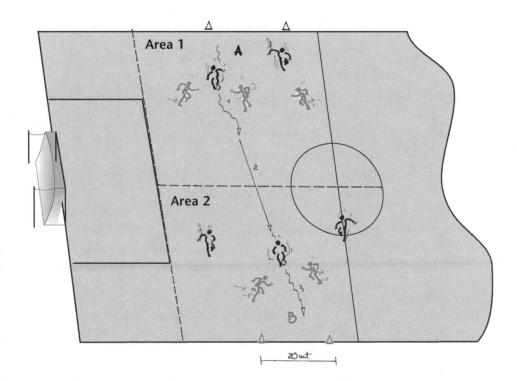

Exercise n. 19

Players
16 + 2 goalkeepers.

Duration
25'.

Objectives
Continuous movement
of players and ball.

Description
Group 6A plays against group 6B on a regular
pitch. The group that gains possession of the
ball or scores has to deliver the ball to a member of its team on the wing.

Variations
1) One team alternates touches.
2) Introduction of two support players who
can shoot at goal.

Exercise n. 20

Players
16 + 2 goalkeepers.

Duration
Every 2 minutes play
ball from one area of
play to the other 6 to 8
times. 2 minute break.

Objectives
Vision of play through
movement of players
and ball.

Description
In area **1** group 4A uses two-touch play to
attack the goal defended by 4B and the keeper.
At the same time group 4B dribbles the ball to
attack the goal defended by group 4A and the
keeper. At R's signal the groups pass the ball to
the opposite area of play and exchange positions.

Variations
1) Speed up exchange of balls between one
area of play and another.
2) Limit touches allowed.
3) 4 against 3 and two support players who act
as playmakers.

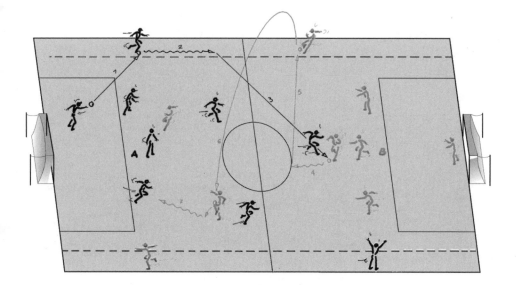

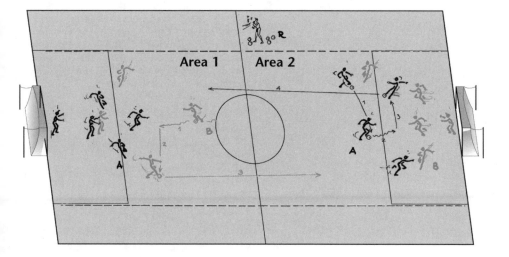

Area 1   Area 2

Exercise n. 21

Players
16.

Duration
15/20 minutes. Change of areas of play every 5 minutes.

Objectives
1) Greater vision of play through an increased movement of players.
2) Flow of movement for co-ordinated precision of shots.

Description
In the 20 x 20 m. boxes marked **1**, **2**, **3** and **4**, groups 2A and 2B battle for possession. They dribble the ball and play 1-2's. At R's signal they exchange balls across a 3 m. space at the center of the area of play. The group that gains possession is attacked by the other group. The exercise is repeated in areas **3** and **4**.

Variations
1) One group plays to keep possession while the other uses pressure play.
2) At R's signal the groups exchange balls with long diagonal passes between areas **1** and **4** and **2** and **3**.
3) A support player who passes the ball between the open spaces.

Exercise n. 22

Players
14.

Duration
15'/20'.

Objectives
Perfection of technique and tactical play.

Description
Groups 7A and 7B play against each other and attempt to get into the box of their opponents' half. They are helped by four players, two from each group who move up and down the wings as far as the halfway line. When these players are in possession of the ball they can only keep it for a maximum of three minutes.

Variations
1) At a signal, a defender joins the attacking players.
2) 8 against 7 and two support players as playmakers.
3) Limited touches, first-time passes and 1-2's.

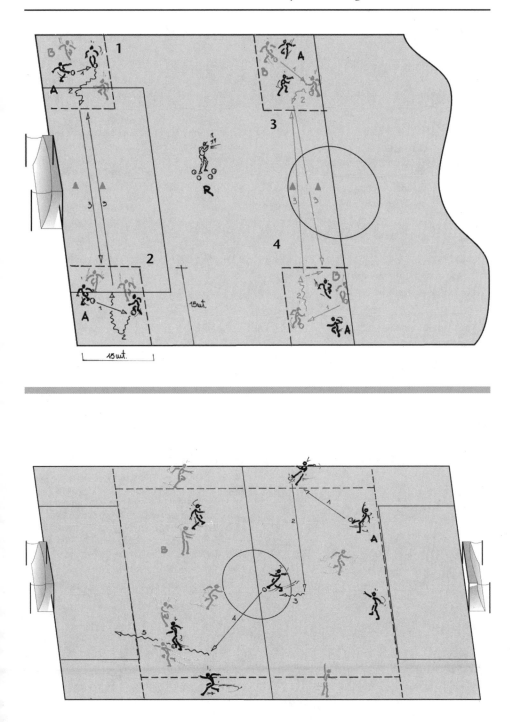

Exercise n. 23

Players
20.

Duration
15 minutes. Exchange of roles every three minutes.

Objectives
Quick exchange of the ball and rapid change of position and play.

Description
In areas **1** and **2** 5A and 5B battle for possession of the ball. In area **1** the ball is to be dribbled, in area **2** two touches are permitted. At R's signal the player in possession in area **1** plays the ball across a 5m. space to his teammates in area **2**. Within one minute all the members of the group must touch the ball before passing it to the opposite area. No player must enter the central area.

Variations
At R's signal the groups exchange balls using long, high passes.

Exercise n. 24

Players
16.

Duration
15/20 minutes. Every two minutes R and K push for change of position in the two areas of play.

Objectives
Development of individual technical skill through collective tactical moves.

Description
In the two 25 x 40 rectangles marked **1** and **2** groups 4A and 4B and 4C and 4D play each other. At R's signal the groups stop play and one of the players of each group moves out of the rectangle to receive a throw from R and K. At the same time the players switch areas of play to receive the ball once again from the player outside the area.

Variations
1) First time passes in areas **1** and **2**.
2) Players outside the areas take the ball into the opposite areas.
3) The players outside the rectangles play the ball into the opposite areas across a 5 m. space.

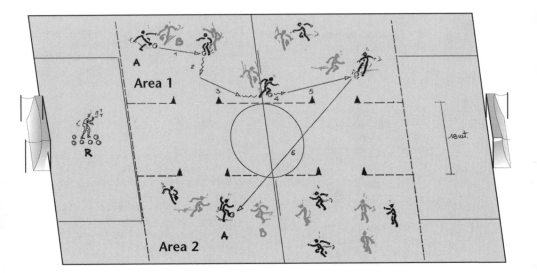

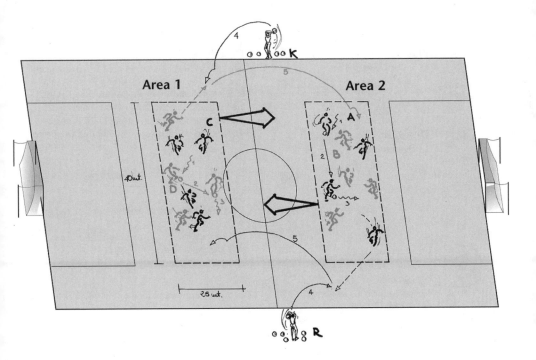

Exercise n. 25

Players
15 + 2 support players
+ 2 goalkeepers.

Duration
15/20 minutes. Switch positions between attacking players and defenders every 5 minutes.

Objectives
Tactical move for support player as playmaker, especially in attacking phase of play.

Description
Groups 8A and 7B play for possession to shoot at the goals defended by the goalkeepers. Players from both groups can only shoot from inside the squares. Only the support players can pass the ball to the players to shoot.

Variations
1) The support player passes in the square, gets the return and shoots.
2) Dribbling and 1-2's are allowed in the square.
3) The team with the greater number of players shoots from outside the square.
4) If a support player is with the attacking group the other defends.

Exercise n. 26

Players
14 + 1 support player
+ 1 goalkeeper.

Duration
2 fifteen minute sessions.

Objectives
1) Quick change of play between one area and another.
2) Play on the wings.

Description
Groups 5A and 5B play in area **1**. After scoring in one of the small goals, group B receives a ball from R and moves to attack the goal in area **2** defended by group 4C and a support player. If group C gains possession it must dribble the ball past area **2** defended by group A.

Variations
1) In area **1** the teams dribble the ball and play 1-2's.
2) The support player can only shoot from outside the penalty area.

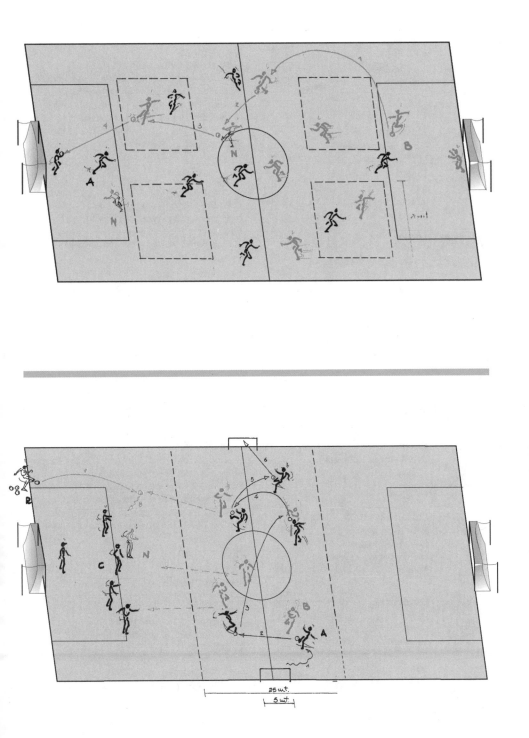

25 ut.

5 ut.

Exercise n. 27

Players
12 + 4 support players.

Duration
4 five minute sessions.

Objectives
Create moves for all players to go for goal.

Description
Groups 6A-6B play each other for possession in the small pitches and go for the small goals in midfield. The support players are the main playmakers and they play long balls and 1-2's to the team in possession of the ball. The team with possession has to shoot at one of the mini-goals in under 2 minutes.

Variations
1) Only long shots can be played.
b. The support players can shoot from the goal line.
2) Play with two balls simultaneously.

Exercise n. 28

Players
16 + 4 support players.

Duration
8/10 three minute session. R pushes for changes of area every minute.

Objectives
1) The support players are the playmakers in the four areas. They create fast moves between players.
2) Organize play covering all areas with rapid movement of players and ball.
3) Rapidly change rhythm of play.

Description
Groups 4A and 4B and 4C and 4D play for possession in the areas 1 and 3. They dribble the ball use 1-2's and move rapidly. At R's signal they move rapidly into areas 2 and 4. Two support players join the groups without the ball and the others play two touch moves and diagonal passes.

Variations
1) 6 against 4 + one playmaker for first time passes.
2) 5 against 3, pressure play.
3) The support player dribbles the ball.
4) Only 1-2's.

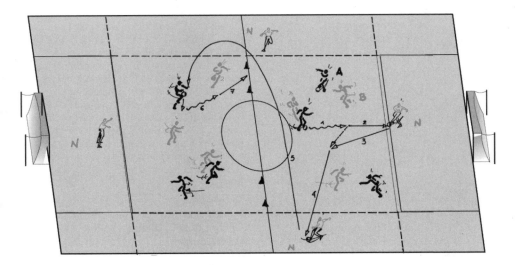

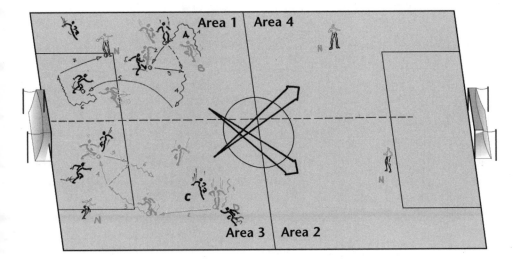

Exercise n. 29

Players
14 + 2 support players + 4 goalkeepers.

Duration
15/20 moves. on goal must be completed inside 2 minutes.

Objectives
1) Control of the ball for follow-up move.
2) Tactical play in area **2** to free the attacking player of the other two areas.

Description
The midfield players 3A and 3B play each other in the central 40 m. area of the pitch. The group in possession must make five passes before giving the ball to their attacking team-mates in areas **1** and **3**. The attacking players must attack the 7 m. goal defended by the goalkeepers, who can only use their feet, and the other group made up of two players. The players in the area out of play move on a ball played by R and the team that gains possession attacks the goal defended by the two keepers and the other group.

Variations
1) The ball is played from area **2** to areas **1** and **3** to the support players who have to finish in under ten seconds.
2) Finish in areas **1** and **3** having beaten the defender with the help of the support player.
3) A goalkeeper plays as a third defender.
4) Limit the touches in area **2**.

Exercise n. 30

Players
12 + 2 support players + 4 goalkeepers.

Duration
Three 5 minute session. Change of positions between groups every 5 minutes.

Objectives
Changes of position and passing for fast moves on goal.

Description
Groups 6A and 6B play for possession in the reduced pitch. They play three-touch moves and 1-2's to shoot inside one minute. The attacking group must play a 1-2 with the support player before shooting at goal. The support players play from the corners of the penalty area.

Variations
1) The support players act as playmakers and cover the whole pitch.
2) Long passes.
3) Finishing headers.
4) When the defenders gain possession they pass the ball to one of the support players and change position.
5) First time passing.

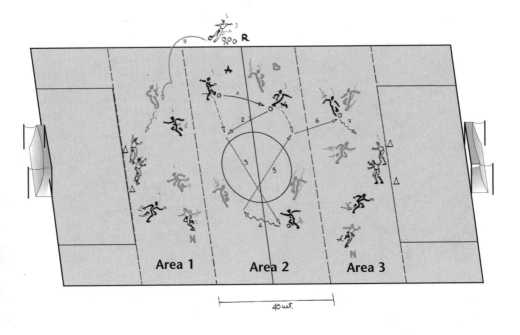

Area 1 **Area 2** **Area 3**

40 mt.

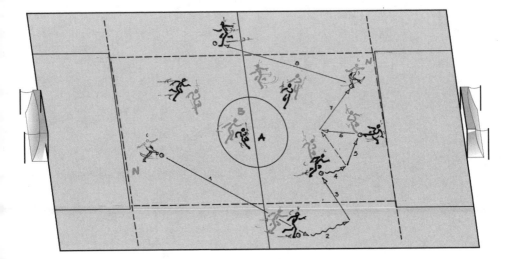

Exercise n. 31

Players
14 + 2 support players.

Duration
5 five minute sessions.

Objectives
The support players keep the play moving with long balls to the wings.

Description
Group 7A plays group 7B for possession on a reduced pitch without any goals. The players use 1-2 combinations when passing the ball. The two support players play on the side of the team in possession and play long balls to the wings.

Variations
1) The support players play on the wings.
2) One team plays with varied combinations, the other is restricted to playing 1-2's.
3) Limited touches.
4) The support players are substituted by the team players.

Exercise n. 32

Players
12 + 2 support players + 2 goalkeepers.

Duration
15'/20'.

Objectives
1) Play concentrated on the player inside the area indicated and on his movement.
2) Development of the technical ability of the player in the designated area.

Description
Group 7A plays group 7B for possession. A player from each team plays inside the area indicated in the diagram of the opponents' area of play. He is not marked and plays long balls for 1-2's.

Variations
1) A player from each team plays in the indicated area.
2) The neutral players shoot from outside the area.

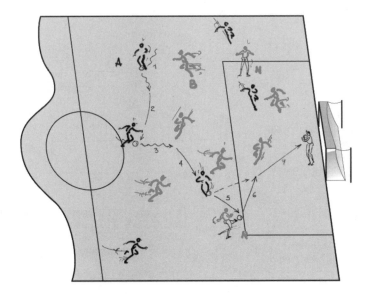

Exercise n. 33

Players
16.

Duration
15/20 minutes. R calls for passing of the ball from one area of play to another to speed up the play.

Objectives
Series of individual moves for basic tactical play.

Description
4A plays 4B for possession in area **1** of the pitch. The two teams combine first time passes and dribbling of the ball. The attacking team carries the ball over an area of 15-meters on the wing. The same exercise is carried out in area **2** of the pitch. No player must enter the center-field area of the pitch. At R's signal the players play long balls to one another.

Variations
1) A support player plays in each field and plays the ball to the opposite field.
2) Two players from each group play two-touch moves while another two use first time passes.
3) At R's signal a player from one group moves to the other group to play 5 against 3.
4) A support player plays in goal. He must only use his feet to defend the goal.
5) At R's signal the player in possession moves from one area of play to another.

Exercise n. 34

Players
20.

Duration
Five 5 minute sessions.

Objectives
1) The players pass the ball using the full width of the field.
2) The defender on the goal line is chosen from between the defenders and the attacking players.

Description
Group 3B plays three-touch and attempts to take the ball over the goal line which is defended by group 2A and a goalkeeper who can only use his feet to save. A similar exercise is repeated in areas **2**, **3**, and **4**. In area **2** a goalkeeper and group 2B defend the goal from group 3A who play two- touch moves. In area **3** group 1A defends with a keeper, group 2B attacks using a series of 1-2 combinations. In area **4** a keeper and group 1B defend the goal from group 2A who dribble the ball.

Variations
1) A playmaker in each attacking group.
2) The attacking players effect three 1-2 combinations before moving off the goal line.
3) Only dribbling of the ball is allowed.
4) Train the attacking players with the defenders.

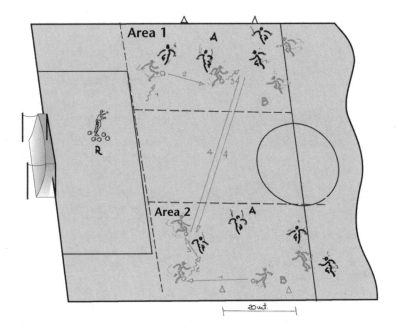

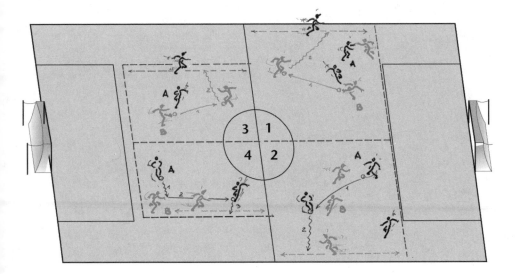

Exercise n. 35

Players
10 + 4 support players.

Duration
Three 10 minute sessions with a 1 minute break.

Objectives
Intensify movement with passing from one side of the pitch to the other.

Description
5A plays 5B for possession on a reduced pitch. They must only use two touches. Four support players play in the areas indicated in the diagram. They play first time passing to the players in possession of the ball. At R's signal the support players can pass the ball to one another to speed up play.

Variations
1) 6 against 6 with three support players.
2) Limit touches allowed.
3) Switch the support players with the players of each group.

Exercise n. 36

Players
17 + 1 support player.

Duration
15/20 minutes. The keepers alternate with their teammates.

Objectives
1) Improve the game with short direct passes.
2) Tactical play to cover all areas of the field.

Description
Group 8A plays group 9B for possession on a reduced pitch. They attempt to dribble the ball across the 16-meter areas opposite them which are defended by two players and a goalkeeper who is only allowed to defend the goal with his feet.

Variations
1) One team plays to keep possession while the other attacks the 16-meter area.
2) Limit touches allowed.
3) Move the extra player from one group to another.

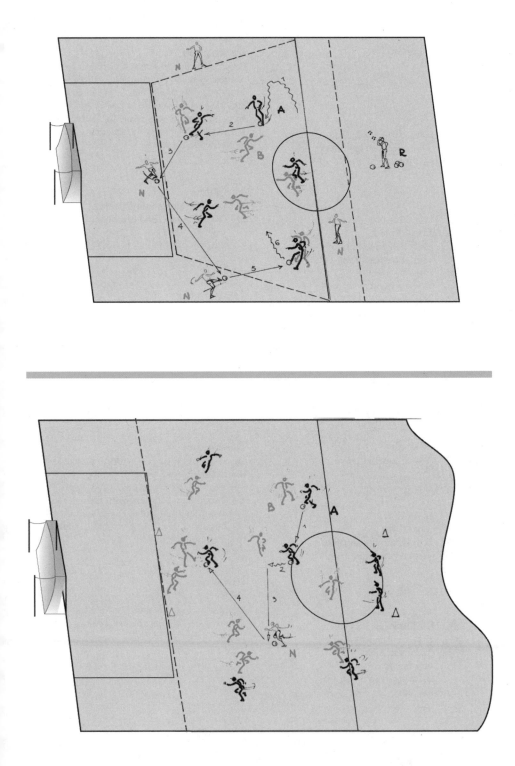

Exercise n. 37

Players
10 + 2 support players.

Duration
Five 5 minute sessions. A 2 minute break.

Objectives
1) Development of individual tactics for marking and tackling.
2) Movement of the ball and players.

Description
Groups 5A and 5B play for possession on a reduced pitch. One group plays three-touch. The two support players stand on the wings and play with the team in possession. At R's signal the two groups leave the ball to move on K and Z's throw from the touchline. Z and K alternate long throws.

Variations
1) Open play or first time passing.
2) 1-2 combination and dribbling.

Exercise n. 38

Players
10 + 2 support players.

Duration
5 three minute sessions with a two minute break.

Objectives
1) Tactical moves of the players in open spaces on the pitch.
2) Each group opens up the game.

Description
On a reduced pitch two support players combine with groups 5A and 5B who play each other for possession on a reduced pitch. The two support players play with the team in possession. They play on the wings and use 1-2 combinations, first time passes and dribbling to speed up the play.

Variations
1) The support players change positions with the players in the teams every 3 minutes.
2) One team dribbles the ball and the other plays three touch football.

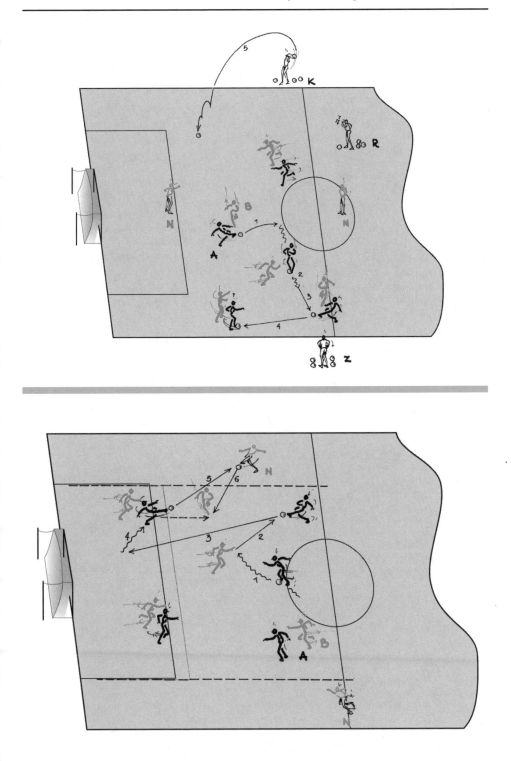

Exercise n. 39

Players
6 + 1 support player.

Description
Group 3A plays group 3B for possession on a reduced pitch. The support player delivers short passes and is the only player allowed to shoot at goal.

Duration
15/20 minutes. Change of groups and support player every 2 minutes.

Variations
1) The support player dribbles and shoots at goal.
2) At R's signal one group is substituted by another during play.
3) One player from each group covers the whole field and acts as playmaker.
4) One player plays two-touch.
5) One player plays on the wing and the other two in the center of the pitch.

Objectives
Tactical play focused on support player who uses first time passes and 1-2 combinations.

Exercise n. 40

Players
18 + 2 support players + 2 goalkeepers.

Description
Group 9A plays group 9B. Group 9A plays only three-touch. Groups 1A and 2B and 2A and 1B play inside the 20 x 30 m. areas. Each group attacks the opponent's area with one player inside the indicated area. This player dribbles past the two defenders to finish. The support players play with the group in possession without entering the indicated areas.

Duration
25/30 minutes continuous play.

Objectives
1) Dribble free of the defenders to finish.
2) Perfection of individual technique.

Variations
1) 2 attacking players and one defender inside the rectangles.
2) The support players shoot from outside the area, the ball is passed to them from the player inside the rectangle.

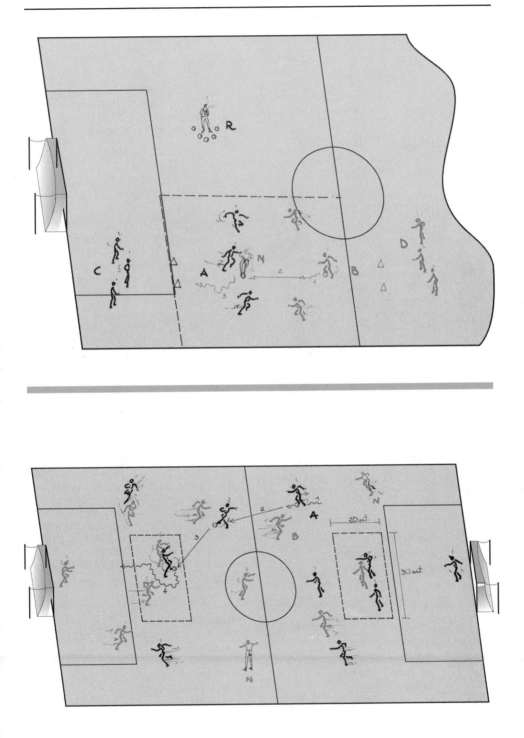

Exercise n. 41

Players
14 + 2 support players.

Duration
8 five minute sessions and a 1 minute pause.

Objectives
Improvement of individual technique through team play.

Description
Group 7A plays group 7B for possession on a reduced pitch. The players of each group play inside 18 x 18 m. areas. The ball must be kept moving with a series of 1-2's etc. played between the players inside the areas and their teammates.

Variations
1) The players inside the areas play one or two touch.
2) The player inside the indicated area can move out with the ball and he is replaced immediately by a player of the same group.

Exercise n. 42

Players
14 + 2 support players.

Duration
Five 6 minute sessions with a 1 minute break.

Objectives
Series of individual moves and team play for basic tactics.

Description
Groups A and B play each other in the reduced pitches **1** and **2**. They are to dribble the ball. Group 4A and group 3B play on pitch **1** while group 4B and group 3A play on pitch **2**. At R's signal the player from each group in possession of the ball moves to the opponents' field followed by all the players from the two groups. The support players keep the dribbling moving.

Variations
1) The support player dribbles the ball from one pitch to the other.
2) Two-touch.
3) First time passing.

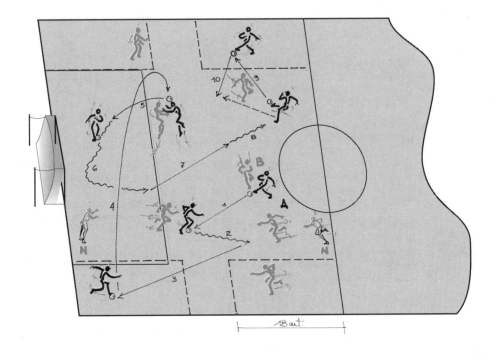

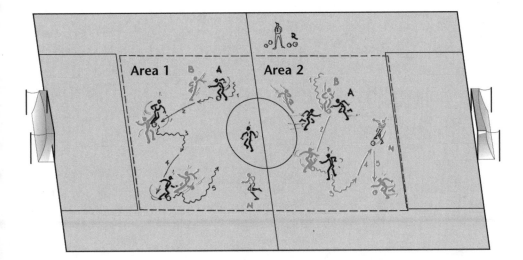

Exercise n. 43

Players
10.

Duration
15 minute sessions.

Objectives
Tactical move to shift play from one end of the field to the other as quickly as possible.

Description
Groups 5A and 5B play each other on a small pitch. Both groups are in possession of a ball. Each group attacks the opponent's goal and defends its own.

Variations
1) One group finishes with straight shots, the other with diagonal shots.
2) At R's signal the two groups exchange balls.
3) When one group gains possession it plays two-touch without shooting at goal.

Exercise n. 44

Players
10 + 3 support players.

Duration
Five to six 5 minute sessions.

Objectives
1) Co-ordinated dynamic move for constant rhythm of play.
2) Rapid passing and changes of position.

Description
Groups 5A and 5B play each other for possession on a small pitch. They pass the ball over one of the 5-meter hurdles placed in a triangular form in three areas of the pitch. Three support players move along the three edges of the areas and play first time touches.

Variations
1) The support player receives the ball and moves into play to substitute the player he received the pass from.
2) At R's signal the players from one group play the ball across the three open spaces in under 1 minute.
3) Each group has a playmaker.

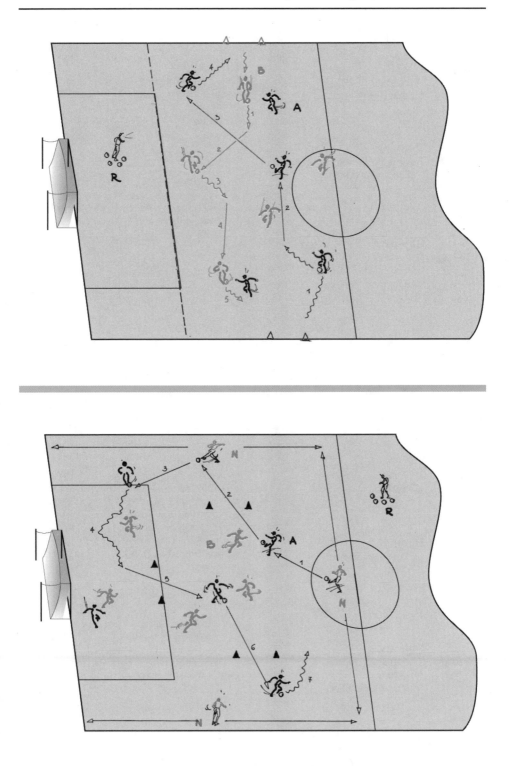

Exercise n. 45

Players
10 + 1 support player
+ 1 goalkeeper.

Duration
4/6 minute sessions
with a 1 minute break.

Objectives
Vision of play and
improvement of indi-
vidual skills.

Description
Group 5A plays group 5B. At R's signal the
group in possession attacks the goals defended
by the other group and the goalkeeper. The
keeper throws the ball out for play.

Variations
1) 4 against 4 with 2 goalkeepers.
2) The keeper can move into attack and is
replaced by the support player.

Exercise n. 46

Players
8 + 2 support players
+ 2 goalkeepers.

Duration
15/20 minute sessions.

Objectives
Co-ordinated dynamic
move to maintain con-
stant rhythm in play.

Description
On a 40 x 60 m. pitch groups 4A and 4B play
each other for possession. They are to shoot on
the mini goals defended by the goalkeepers in
a time of under 40 seconds. The two support
players keep the dribbling of the ball moving
and play first time passes and 1-2's. The goalkeepers from each group move into fast attacking moves.

Variations
1) Each group replaces its goalkeeper with an
attacker after each move in attack.
2) The support players only play long crosses
for the attacking players to head the ball.

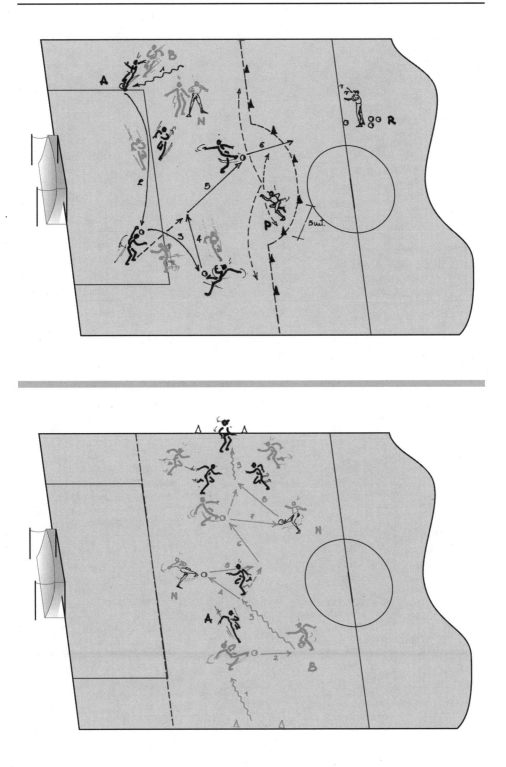

Exercise n. 47

Players
11 + 2 goalkeepers.

Duration
Five to six 3 minute sessions. A 1 minute break.

Objectives
Tactical play for the team attacking the goal, the other group concentrates on defending the goal and maintaining possession.

Description
On a small pitch group 6A plays three-touch soccer to maintain possession and defend the 5-meter goal mouth. Group 4B attacks the goal, the players dribble the ball and play 1-2's. At R's signal a player from group A comes into play from behind one of the goals and plays exclusively as a defender for a 20 minute period.

Variations
1) The keepers join in the play to maintain possession.
2) A fifth player from group B acts as playmaker.
3) Quick breaks in attack from one goal to another, long passes and dummies.
4) Replace defenders with attackers every three minutes etc.

Exercise n. 48

Players
4 + 1 support player.

Duration
15 minutes. Group should be replaced every three minutes and their roles switched every minute.

Objectives
Tactical play with 1-2's and dribbling of the ball.

Description
Groups 2A and 2B dribble the ball, tackle and play 1-2's for possession on a small pitch. they shoot on the 2-meter goals. the support player plays short fast passes to keep the game moving. At R's signal the groups continue play with three-touches.

Variations
1) One player is designated to shoot at goal.
2) At R's signal an extra player moves into one of the groups.
3) Build-up of play with vertical passes.
4) The player in possession of the ball is attacked by both players from the other group.
5) The support player plays with the group that doesn't have the ball.

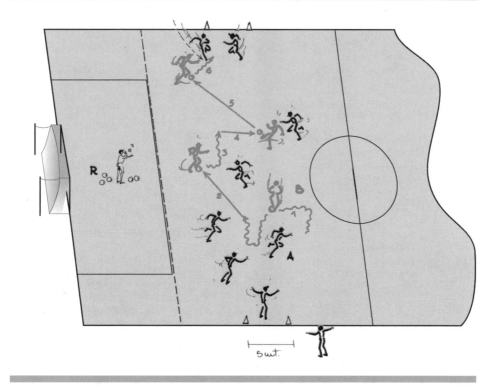

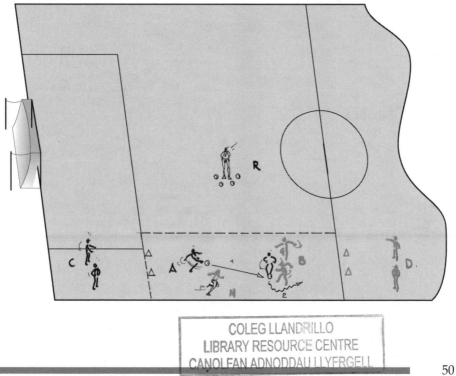

Exercise n. 49

Players
6 + 1 support players.

Duration
Five 5 minute sessions.
Change of groups after
every two moves.

Objectives
Tactical play with
dribbling and 1-2's.

Description
Groups 3A and 3B play each other for possession on a small pitch with mini goals. Once
they gain possession they have to shoot in
under a minute. The support player assists the
group in possession of the ball with first time
passes and 1-2's.

Variations
1) The support player only plays in midfield.
2) The team in possession must play at least
five passes before shooting on goal.
3) 4 against 3 with only the support player
being allowed to shoot on goal.
4) The team that manages to score two to three
times in a row attacks both of the goals assisted by the support player and the other team
defends.

Exercise n. 50

Players
14 + 2 support players
+ 2 goalkeepers.

Duration
25 minutes of continu-
ous play.

Objectives
Creative play for attack-
ing moves.

Description
Groups 7A and 7B play each other for possession. The team in possession has to dribble the
ball across a 5-meter space inside the opponents' half of the field and players of the
attacking group must be inside the opponents'
half.

Variations
1) Only the support players can shoot at goal.
2) Move the play from one side of the pitch to
the other.

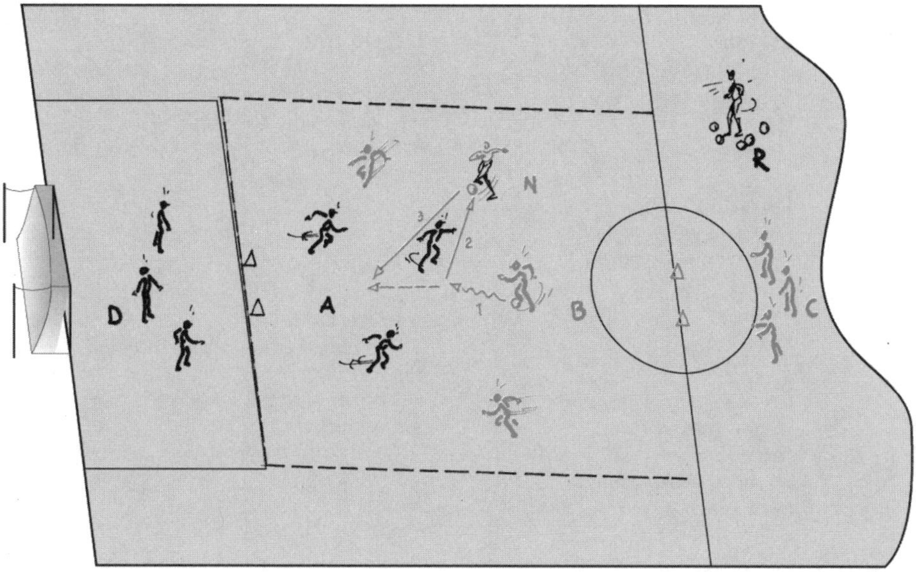
N
R
D
A
B
C
1
2
3

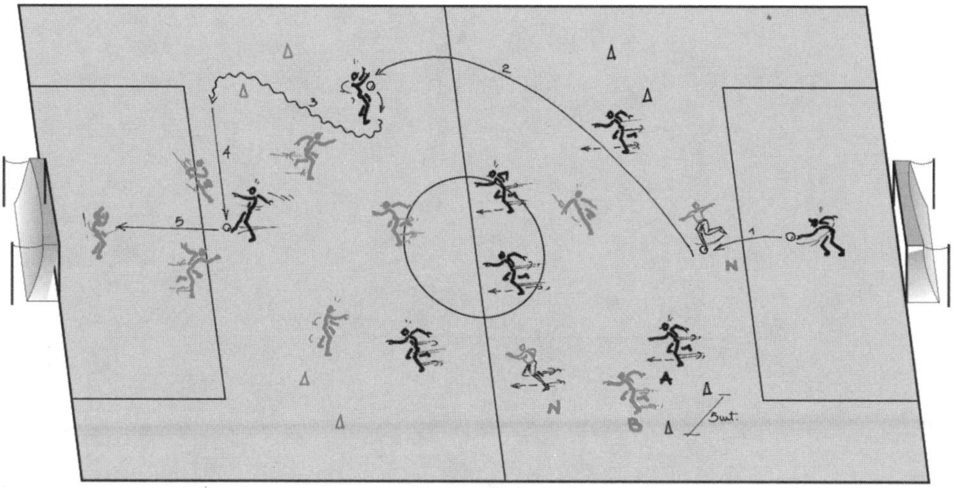
1
2
3
4
5
N
A
B

Exercise n. 51

Players
14 + 2 support players
+ 2 goalkeepers.

Duration
Five 6 minute sessions
with a 2 minute break.

Objectives
Rapid movement of
players and ball using
the wings.

Description
Groups 7A and 7B play each other for possession. They attack each others' goal without
moving into the areas indicated by the dotted
line. The support players assist play from the
wings.

Variations
1) The indicated areas have different forms and
numbers.
2) The support players only play long balls
across the indicated areas.
3) No support players.

CHAPTER TWO

Changes of position for improvement of technique and tactics for vision of play

1) Exercises in different forms
2) Precision and perfection of shots
3) Play in both directions
4) Play on the wings

These exercises are devised in such a way that they become gradually more difficult to satisfy the more demanding situations of play.

The player develops confidence to face ever more difficult game situations.

The player must link different spontaneous movements to create dynamic combinations. The player finds himself in a situation which requires adaptation to a multiplicity of situations regarding time and space.

The exercise will be applied according to the judgement of the trainer and the amount of exercises will depend on the requirements of the player regarding his physical and technical ability.

Exercise n. 52

Players
10 + 2 goalkeepers.

Duration
8/10 attacking moves for each group for 20 minutes.

Objectives
1) Make play for the sweeper, both in defensive and attacking moves.
2) Alternation in attack with change of position between attackers and defenders.

Description
On the small pitch marked **1**, group 5A attacks the goal playing two-touch soccer. The goal is defended by group 5B and a goalkeeper. Group A must shoot at goal in under a minute. Most shots should be form the wings. Group B plays with a sweeper and plays attacking soccer. After finishing group B attacks the goal on pitch **2** defending by group A. Every three minutes other groups alternate the play.

Variations
1) A support player starts the attack from one half of the field to the other.
2) Limit the touches allowed.
3) 6 against 4 + 2 support players.
4) The goalkeeper assists play, handling the ball outside the goal.
5) The team in attack has to conclude within 30 seconds once it has passed the half-way line.

Exercise n. 53

Players
12 + 2 support players + 2 goalkeepers.

Duration
15/20 minutes. Change of positions between attackers and defenders every five minutes.

Objectives
1) Attacking play mainly from the wings.
2) Concentration on support player to assist fast attacking moves.
3) Make use of the whole field and dribble free of the opponent.

Description
Groups 6A and 6B play each other to attack the goal on a small pitch. The two support players assist moves to speed up the play and create shooting chances along with the three attacking players.

Variations
1) Play concentrated on 1-2's.
2) Before shooting at goal all the players from the attacking group must be beyond the halfway line.
3) Build-up of the attack with only diagonal passes.
4) The attack is built up with two playmakers who can't shoot.
5) Only the support players shoot at goal.

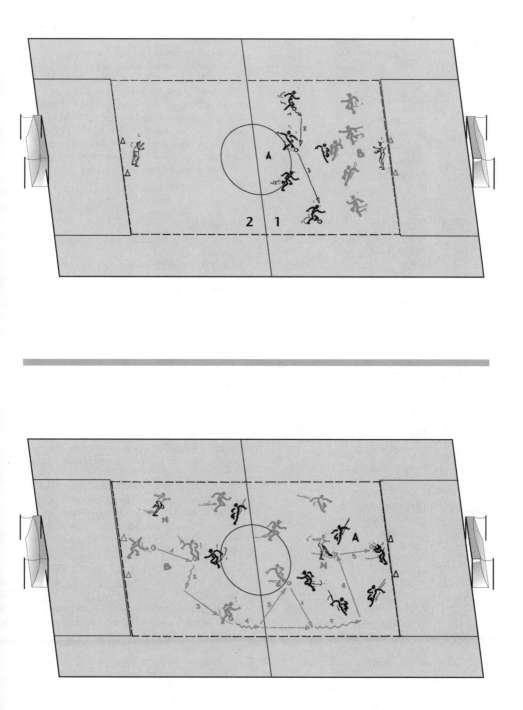

Exercise n. 54

Players
15 + 2 goalkeepers.

Duration
18 minutes with a 1 minute break. Switch positions of the two groups every 6 minutes.

Objectives
1) Each group builds up its attack along the wings.
2) The rapid interchange between 2 attackers and 2 defenders during the move creates conclusive tactical play.

Description
Group 5B moves from the halfway line to attack the goal defended by the goalkeeper and group 5A.
They must finish on goal within 2 minutes. At R's signal two attacking players from group B change positions with two defenders from group A. When the move has finished group A attacks the goal defended by the goalkeeper and group 5C. When the move is over group C attacks the goal defended by group B and so on.

Variations
1) Two touches for the attackers and three for the defenders.
2) A support player assists play from along the wings.
3) If the defending team gains possession it has to try to maintain possession for 2 minutes.
4) Each attacking team must lose defenders and dribble the ball.

Exercise n. 55

Players
14 + 2 goalkeepers.

Duration
Change of position between attackers and defenders every five minutes. 15/20 minutes of play.

Objectives
1) Tactical move aimed at creating vertical movement up and down the field.
2) The area indicated by the dotted line for the shot forces the attacker to dribble free of his opponent.

Description
Groups 7A and 7B play each other for possession to attack and finish on goal within 2 minutes.
The attacking group must build up its attack by carrying the ball across a 30m. space at the center of the field, to shoot at goal from the area indicated by the dotted line. The goalkeepers move out of their penalty areas to assist play.

Variations
1) The defenders must pass the ball to each other several times before moving into attack so as to force their opponents to try to regain possession.
2) A support player plays in the indicated area to assist dribbling moves and 1-2's before shots on goal.
3) Attack on goal in under a minute.

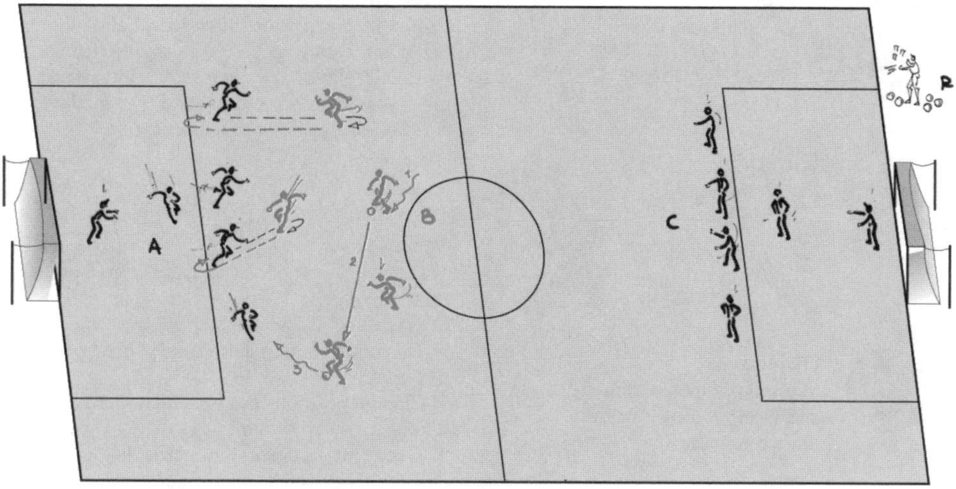
A
B
C
R

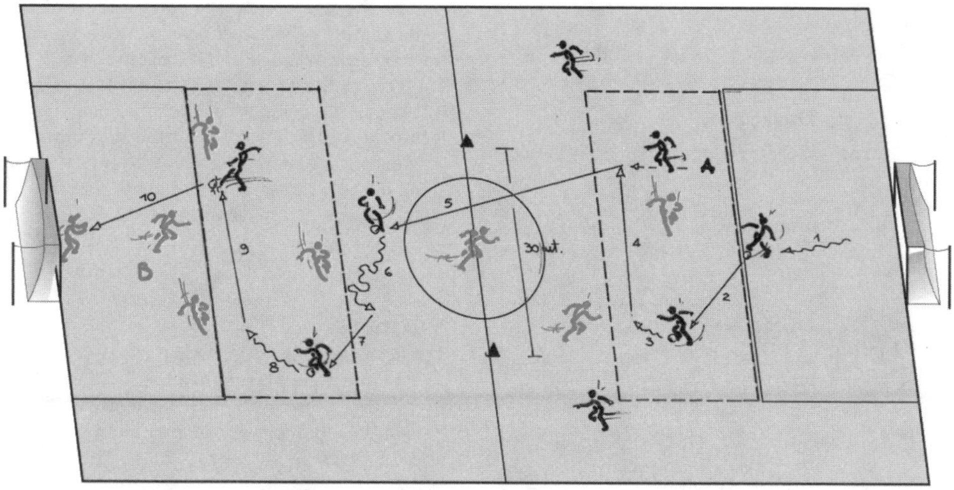
A
B
30 mt.

Exercise n. 56

Players
12 + 1 goalkeeper.

Duration
15/20 minutes.

Objectives
Maintaining possession and freeing oneself from one's opponent.

Description
Group 6A plays three-touch soccer and defends the 4-meter goal on a small pitch. Group 6B plays two-touch soccer and attacks the goal which is also defended by a goalkeeper who is only allowed to use his feet.

Variations
1) Designate one player to shoot at goal on each move.
2) Play two 1-2's before each shot.
3) The attackers play with two balls when dribbling.
4) Change positions between attackers and defenders every two minutes.
5) The group in possession of the ball attacks and the other defends.

Exercise n. 57

Players
8 + 2 support players.

Duration
Five 5 minute sessions. Move from one area to another every five minutes.

Objectives
1) Tactical play for a build-up to shot moving from one small vertical area to a larger horizontal area.
2) Play concentrated on movements of players and ball.

Description
Groups 4A and 4B play each other for possession on the small pitch. They attack the 3-meter goals and play short, fast passes. At R's signal the two groups move into the bigger area **2**. They attack the 4 meter goals co-ordinated by two support players who move into play once R throws the ball into play for the start of the new exercise. The two support players do not shoot on goal but act as playmakers both in attacking and defensive moves.

Variations
1) After 6/8 shots in the bigger area a defender and an attacking player are added.
2) In area **1** passes and diagonal shots.
3) Bring the ball forward in area **2** and shoot when R gives the signal.

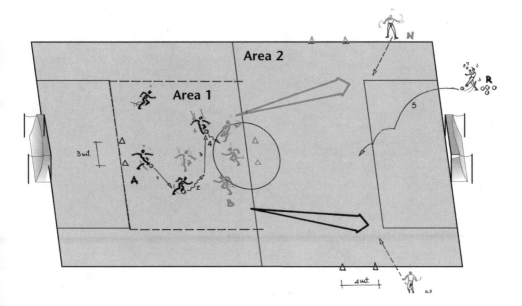

Exercise n. 58

Players
10 + 2 support players + 2 goalkeepers.

Duration
Five 5 minute sessions. Every five minutes attackers and defenders of the same group change positions.

Objectives
1) Fast exchanges with rapid changes of position and play.
2) Rapid build-up of moves in attack.

Description
Group 2B attacks the goal defended by group 3A and the goalkeeper on the small pitch marked **1**. Group 2A attacks the goal defended by group 3B and the goalkeeper on pitch **2**. The defenders of each group play the ball to their attacking teammates on the opposite pitch via the support player who plays the ball on with long passes from off the pitch. The defenders are limited to three touches. The attacking moves on goal are to be finished inside 2 minutes with a shot.

Variations
1) Limit touches.
2) The support player can only come onto the pitch with the attacking players to shoot at goal.
3) 3 against 3 + 4 support players (two on one pitch and two off the wings.)

Exercise n. 59

Players
9 + 1 goalkeeper.

Duration
Two 10 minute sessions. Change positions between attackers and defenders every 5 minutes.

Objectives
Tactical play for rapid movement of players and ball.

Description
Group 3A dribbles the ball and plays 1-2's to attack the goal defended by the goalkeeper and group 4B who plays three-touch soccer. When group A enters the 30-meter area 1A and 1B move onto the field and start to assist their respective groups once they have passed the 30 meter mark.

Variations
1) The defender B moves into play as a sweeper and the attacker A as a striker from outside the area.
2) The goalkeeper plays outside the goals as a defender.
3) During play a defender becomes an attacker and vice versa.

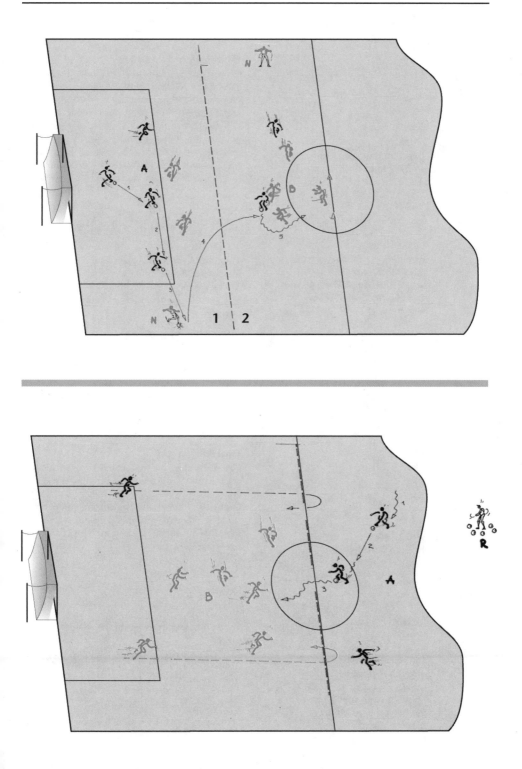

Exercise n. 60

Players
7 + 1 goalkeeper.

Duration
Two 10 minute sessions with a 2 minute break.

Description
Group 2A attacks the goal defended by group 4B and the goalkeeper. When group 2A gets past the dotted line which designates the 30-meter mark two other players come into play to assist them. Once the two new players have got past the 30-meter mark they play two-touch soccer to attack goal. If group B gains possession it takes the ball over the 30-meter line to attack the goal defended by group 4A.

Objectives
By entering and leaving the 30 meter area players are forced to move and play the ball over wider spaces.

Variations
1) Group A can shoot when all the players are inside the 30-meter area.
2) The defenders play with a sweeper.
3) Alternate the defenders with the attacking players.

Exercise n. 61

Players
15 + 2 goalkeepers.

Duration
15/20 minutes.

Description
Group 7A and 7B play each other on a full size pitch to attack the goals defended by the keepers.

Group A attacks with long crosses and conclusive headers while group B concentrates on long driving shots, building up the play along the wings.

Objectives
1) Tactics for defensive and attacking play through individual skills.
2) Cover open spaces on the pitch caused by the reduced number of players.

Variations
1) The goalkeeper assists in the attack with group A.
2) Shots exclusively from outside the area.
3) 10 against 10 with 2 neutral players whose roles are as playmakers.

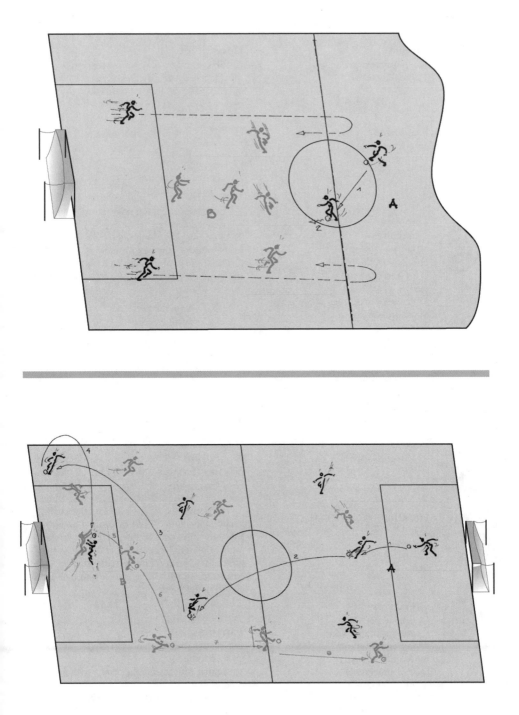

Exercise n. 62

Players
12 + 1 support player
+ 2 goalkeepers.

Duration
6/8 five minute
sessions.

Description
Group 6A and 6B play for possession to attack the goals defended by the keepers. They are only to play first time passes. The support player plays with the group that doesn't have possession

Objectives
1) The two groups build-up through long, short and diagonal passes.
2) The support player plays pressing.

Variations
1) The groups must not pass the ball to their respective keepers.
2) Attacking play along the wings with crosses to the center of the box for conclusive headers.
3) The support player acts as a playmaker for the group in possession.

Exercise n. 63

Players
18 + 2 goalkeepers.

Duration
15/20 two minute
sessions.

Description
Group 3A and 3B, both in possession of a ball, play first time passes in area **2** of the pitch. At R's signal group A enters area **3** of the pitch with the ball. It plays three-touch soccer and 1-2's to attack the goal defended by the goalkeeper and group 3B. At the same time group B moves into area **1** of the pitch with the ball to repeat the exercise on the goal defended by group 3A. The attacking players in areas **1** and **3** must finish with direct shots from inside the box in under 1 minute.

Objectives
1) Tactical play to respond rapidly to an advantage situation.
2) Defenders' objective to stop attackers moving in to shoot.
3) The group with numerical superiority spreads out over the pitch and moves deep into the opponent's half.

Variations
1) Alternate the 3 defenders with the attackers every 2 minutes.
2) Limited touches for the group with numerical superiority.
3) Shot at goal after two 1-2 combinations.

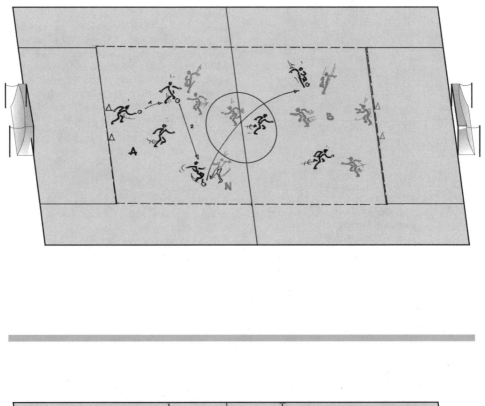

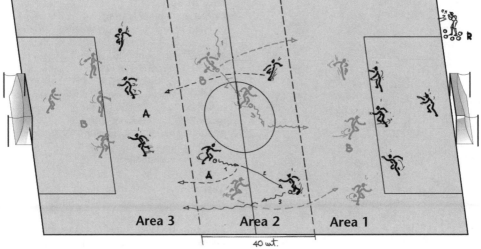

Area 3 | Area 2 | Area 1

40 mt.

Exercise n. 64

Players
20.

Duration
Two 10 minute sessions.

Description
Groups 5A and 5B play each other for possession on the small pitches **1** and **2**. They play three-touch soccer and shoot at goal. When 1 player loses possession he stands in the corner of the pitch and the play continues until a goal is scored. At R's signal the groups from the two opposite areas exchange balls with a long pass to carry on the play dribbling the ball and pressing to finish on goal.

Objectives
1) Control with rapid exchanges of the ball to finish with low, hard drives at goal.
2) Tactical play 1 against 1 with emphasis on the final pass.

Variations
1) Pass to player on the run and low driving shot at goal.
2) Passes and diagonal shots.
3) At R's signal the players in possession of the ball take it into the opponent's area to carry on the play 6 against 4.

Exercise n. 65

Players
14 + 2 goalkeepers.

Duration
20 minutes. Every 5 minutes the players from each group change positions.

Description
On the small pitch **1**, group 3A dribbles the ball and attacks the goal defended by group 4B. In area **2**, the same exercise is repeated with group 3B playing attacking soccer and group 4A defending. At R's signal groups 4A and 3B move rapidly from area **2** to area **1** leaving the ball behind them. They join their teammates to form two teams, 7A and 7B. the game continues with R throwing a new ball into play, the group that gains possession attacks the opponent's goal and has to shoot in under 30 seconds from outside the area.

Objectives
Tactical adaptation to attacking and defensive play.

Variations
1) Diagonal passes and shots from a central position.
2) A support player comes onto the pitch as a defender.
3) During the second part of the exercise the attacking player shoots after dribbling the ball.
4) The striker moves in to strike a low, hard ball.

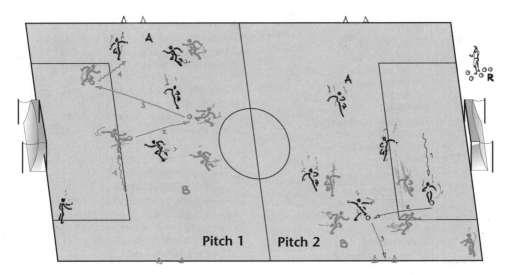

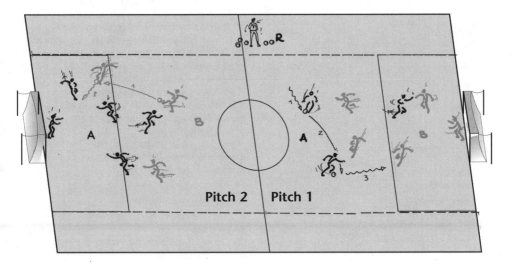

Exercise n. 66

Players
16 + 2 goalkeepers.

Duration
Five 5 minute sessions.
Every 5 minutes the
players change posi-
tions.

Objectives
1) Tactical move for
rapid play and first time
passing.
2) Fast control of the
ball for rapid finishing
on goal.
3) Fast cross for striker
who runs into position
to strike a low drive at
goal.

Description
Groups 4A and 4B dribble and press to shoot
on the small 5-meter goals defended by the
goalkeepers. At the same time in the smaller
area **2** groups A and B play for possession to
shoot on the small 2 meter goals without keepers. At R's signal the groups in each area leave
the ball and follow a throw from R. The shot is
to be taken in rotation by each of the 4 players.

Variations
1) Fast 1-2 combinations before shot.
2) One playmaker who can't shoot at goal.
3) Fast straight and angled passing of the ball.
4) 4 defenders and 5 attacking players for
decisive finishing
5) Limit touches allowed.

Exercise n. 67

Players
18 + 2 goalkeepers.

Duration
15/20 moves for 90
minutes.

Description
Group 3B plays attacking soccer and group 2A
defends in area **1** of the pitch. Groups 4A and
4B play centerfield in the 30 meter area marked
2. Groups 3A and 2B respectively play attack
and defense in area **3** of the pitch. The move
starts from area **1** of the pitch with the two A
defenders who pass the ball to their midfield
team-mates in area **2** of the field. These play
the ball on to the 3A attack to finish in area **3**. If
possession is gained in one of the areas by
group B the direction of the attack changes
with group A defending following the same
pattern as before. The move is to be completed
inside 30 seconds.

Objectives
Fast moves to allow
attack to move free of
defense.

Variations
1) One team plays in attack and the other tries
to keep possession.
2) Change of position for each group in each
area every three minutes.
3) Seven against seven with long crosses from
the wings.
4) Very number of touches allowed and speed
of play in the various areas.
5) At R's signal the players from areas **1** and **3**
switch positions.

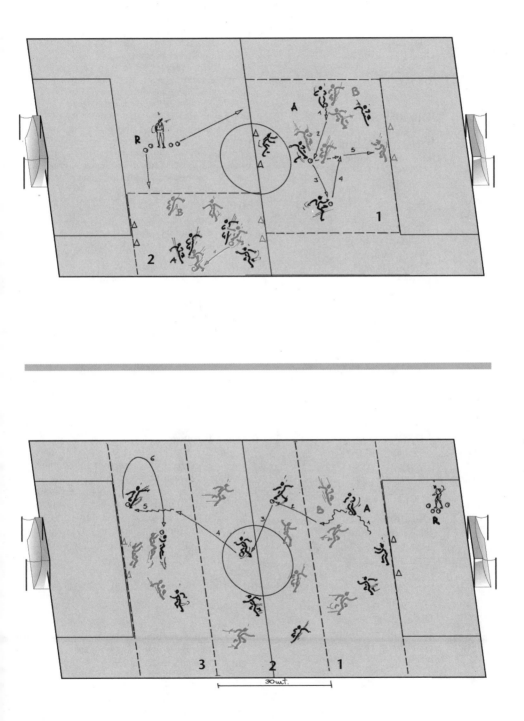

Exercise n. 68

Players
20 + 1 support player
+ 2 goalkeepers.

Duration
Five 5 minute sessions.
Change positions of the
attackers, centerfield
players and defenders
every 5 minutes.

Objectives
1) Tactical play for
direct moves using all
the space in each area
for first time passing,
dribbling and pressing.
2) Defensive tactics to
gain possession and get
the attack moving.

Description
In area **1** group 4B plays defensive soccer while
group 3A attacks. In area **2** groups 2A and 2B play
centerfield with a support player. In area **3** of the
field group 3B attacks and group 4A defends. In
areas **1** and **3** a player from each group plays on the
wing to assist the attack with first time passes and
long crosses. The game starts from area **1** with
group B who passes the ball to the centerfield
group in area **2** who play it on to their attack in
area **3** to finish. All moves from area **1** to **3** must be
completed inside 1 minute. If the opposing group
gains possession during the move they keep the
ball and the attack moves in the opposite direction
following the numerical order of the areas.

Variations
1) Two-touch in areas **1** and **3**.
2) Only dribbling and pressing in area **2**.
3) The support player can move out of area **2** and
shoot at goal from outside the area.
4) The support player can pass the ball from one
area to the other without respecting the numerical
sequence.
5) The attacking player on the wing can move off
the field and is automatically substituted by a
teammate.
6) One player is designated to shoot at goal in areas
1 and **3**.

Exercise n. 69

Players
10 + 1 support player.

Duration
Six 5 minute sessions.

Objectives
Tactical play for build-
up of fast incisive
moves.

Description
Group 3B plays two-touch soccer and 1-2 combinations in area **1** of the pitch. It attacks the 5-
meter goal defended by group 2A and the
goalkeeper. The same exercise is practiced in
area **2** with group 2B defending and group 3A
attacking. The keepers are only allowed to use
their feet and they join in the play out of goals.
The support player plays first time passes to
keep the play moving.

Variations
1) At R's signal the defenders switch positions
with the attackers in their own area.
2) First time passes with a playmaker who is
not allowed to shoot at goal.

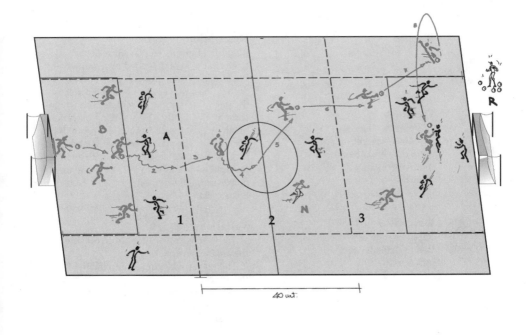

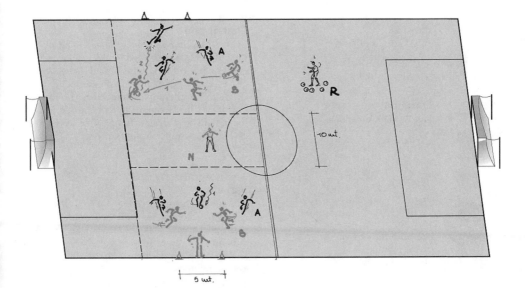

Exercise n. 70

Players
14 + 2 goalkeepers.

Description
In midfield group 4A plays three-touch soccer to attack the goal defended by group 4B and a goalkeeper. When group A goes beyond the dotted line a player from group B comes onto the pitch to assist the defenders. The whole team marks tightly. The attacking players must finish on goal inside 1 minute. If group B gains possession they attack the other goal defended by group 4C and a goalkeeper with another player who comes in to play as a defender. A player from group A joins group B when group B is attacking.

Duration
7/8 moves. Change of positions between defenders and attacking players every 3 minutes.

Objectives
Rapid change of position of defender to attacker.

Variations
1) The defense must shoot from outside the area when attacking.
2) The player who comes onto the field assists the attack.
3) The attacking players play two-touches and fast combination moves.

Exercise n. 71

Players
10 + 1 support player + 2 goalkeepers.

Description
In area **1** group 3B dribbles the ball to attack the 5-meter goal defended by the goalkeeper and group 2A. At the same time the same exercise is carried out in area **2** with group 2B defending and group 3A attacking. The support player in the central 10-meter area assists the play in both areas with first time passes and high crosses for headers at goal.

Duration
Five 5 minute sessions.

Objectives
Speed of play in each area with the support player moving in to play long crosses.

Variations
1) Limit touches allowed.
2) The goalkeeper joins with the defense out of the goal area to make the attack's task more difficult.
3) The defenders alternate with the attackers every 5 minutes.
4) The attacking players play with a playmaker.
5) The 3 attacking players alternate their shots at goal.

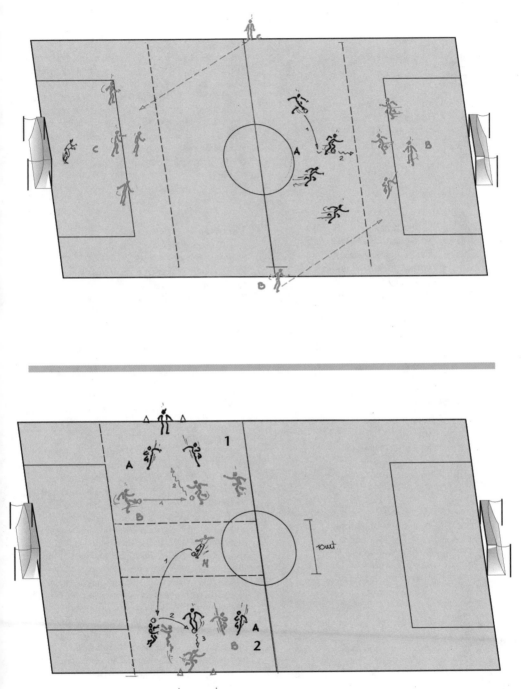

Exercise n. 72

Players
14 + 2 goalkeepers.

Duration
8/10 changes of area every 2 minutes.

Description
Group 3B plays two-touch soccer and 1-2 combinations to attack the goal defended by group 4A and the goalkeeper in area **1**. Group 3A attacks the goal defended by group 4B and the goalkeeper in area **2**. At R's signal the attacking group plays the ball to the defending group with a long pass and the roles are inverted (the groups with 3 players become defenders and the groups with 4 players become attacking players).

Objectives
1) Tactical play to free the player in possession and allow him to finish.
2) Movement of players to cover areas of pitch correctly.

Variations
1) The groups attack with a limited amount of passes allowed.
2) A support player in each area as a playmaker.
3) One player is designated to shoot.

Exercise n. 73

Players
23 + 2 goalkeepers.

Duration
25 minutes of continuous play. The teams exchange areas every 5 minutes with a 1 minute break for the change of area.

Objectives
Tactical move to improve vision and move free of opponent.

Description
Groups A and B play each other for position in areas **1**, **2** and **3**. In area 1 group 2A plays group 2B. The team in possession, dribbling the ball, attacks the two mini-goals defended by the other group. Each group has two players standing at opposite corners of the area who assist in 1-2's, dribbling etc. The support player plays wide balls. Groups 2A and 2B in area **2** play three-touch soccer to shoot at the small goals. They are assisted by two players who stand on the edges of the playing area. The support players should concentrate on first time passes. In area **3** group 4A plays three-touch soccer to defend the mini goals attacked by group 3B. The players in the corners play first time touches to assist the play. Play starts from a throw by R, K, and T to each area.

Variations
1) Exchange of position with players in corners during play.
2) The support players play as playmakers.

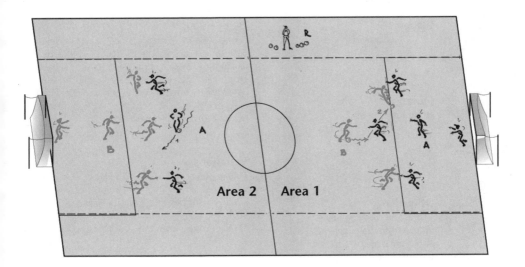

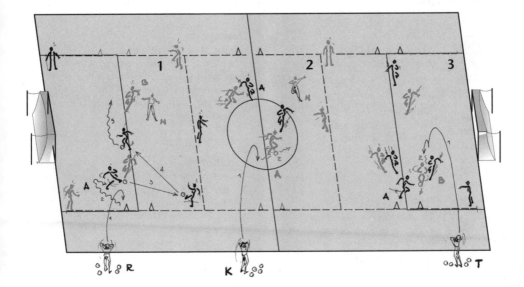

Exercise n. 74

Players
14 + 2 goalkeepers.

Duration
20 minutes.

Objectives
1) Build-up of attacking moves from the edges of the pitch to support the attack.
2) Rapid and continuous changes of play from one side of the field to the other.

Description
Group 3A and 3B play each other in midfield with three-touch soccer, the team in possession has to finish with a shot inside a minute. Each group has 4 players who are confined to designated areas along the edges of the pitch. The 4 players off the field assist play without bringing their own goalkeepers into play.

Variations
1) One player is designated to shoot from the wings.
2) Only a support player is allowed to shoot at goal.
3) One group plays only first time passes.

Exercise n. 75

Players
14 + 2 support players + goalkeepers.

Duration
Five 5 minute sessions with a 2 minute break.

Objectives
The support players are playmakers. They assist the players in the lateral areas creating heading chances.

Description
Groups 5A and 5B play each other in midfield. Two players from each group play inside the areas to the side of the goals and they play crosses for finishing headers. Only the support players play balls for the attacking players in the lateral areas.

Variations
1) 6 defend the two goals and 4 attack.
2) Only the support players are allowed to shoot.
3) One designated player to play first time shots at goal.

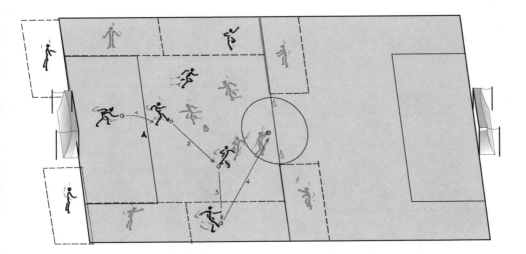

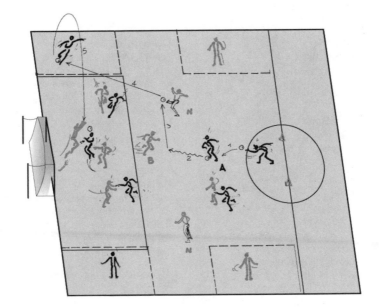

Exercise n. 76

Players
14 + 1 support player + 2 goalkeepers.

Duration
Five 6 minute sessions.

Objectives
Tactical move for speed in attack to create shooting chances for designated player on the wing.

Description
Groups 3A and 3B play for possession in area **1**. They are assisted by groups 4A and 4B (2A against 2B) on the wings. The players in the central area create shooting chances for the players on the wings who have to finish in under 40 seconds.

Variations
1) The support player starts the move with a long ball to the wing.
2) 2 against 2 in area **1** and 3 against 3 on the wings.
3) All players play three-touch soccer.

Exercise n. 77

Players
9 + 2 goalkeepers

Duration
8/10 two minute sessions.

Objectives
Tactical move to capitalize on open spaces and movement of players.

Description
Groups 4A and 3B play on a small pitch to attack the 5-meter goals. Group 4A plays two-touch soccer. During defensive play one player comes onto the field for each group. He leaves the pitch when the move is over.

Variations
1) Group 4A plays all combinations and group 3B plays first time passes.
2) Include 2 support players.
3) 4 players off the pitch (one on each side) to play first time passes.

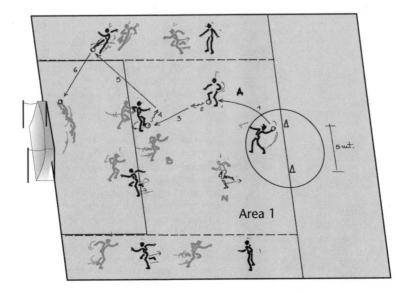

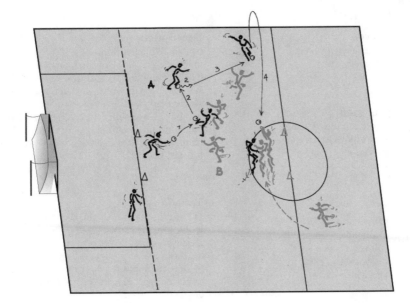

Exercise n. 78

Players
12.

Duration
20 minutes.

Objectives
1) Standardization of attacking play through technical and tactical perfection of players.
2) Capability of adaptation of players to new offensive and defensive tactical play.

Description
Groups 6A and 6B play each other on a small pitch to attack the goals 1 and 2 on the side of the pitch. They are limited to two touches. At R's signal the two groups play all combinations and move the play to the goals 3 and 4 at the center of the pitch and on the edge of the box.

Variations
1) Two-touch soccer for the goals 1 and 2 on the side of the pitch and open play for the goals 3 and 4.
2) At R's signal the groups attack goals 1 and 2 with vertical passes and the goals 3 and 4 with diagonal passes.
3) At R's signal the group with the ball has to effect two 1-2 combinations before shooting when it changes play.
4) At R's signal the group in possession plays first time passes and uses a playmaker who provides headers for the attacking players.
5) At R's signal a player from one group moves to the other to continue play 7 against 5.

Exercise n. 79

Players
8 + 2 support players + 2 goalkeepers.

Duration
15/20 minutes. Change of positions between all players every three minutes.

Objectives
The goalkeepers and the support players are the playmakers for the attack.

Description
In a small pitch groups 3A and 3B play three-touch soccer. They play each other to finish inside 1 minute. The goals are defended by the keepers. Each group is assisted by another player who plays first time passes from the wings. The two support players play 1-2 combinations but cannot play with the two players on the wings. They can pass to the goalkeepers to assist the attack.

Variations
1) The play starts from the keeper and moves to the support player.
2) The support players only play first time touches.
3) Only the support player can shoot at goal.
4) The support players only play with the players on the wings.
5) The two play first time touches and the support players play open soccer.

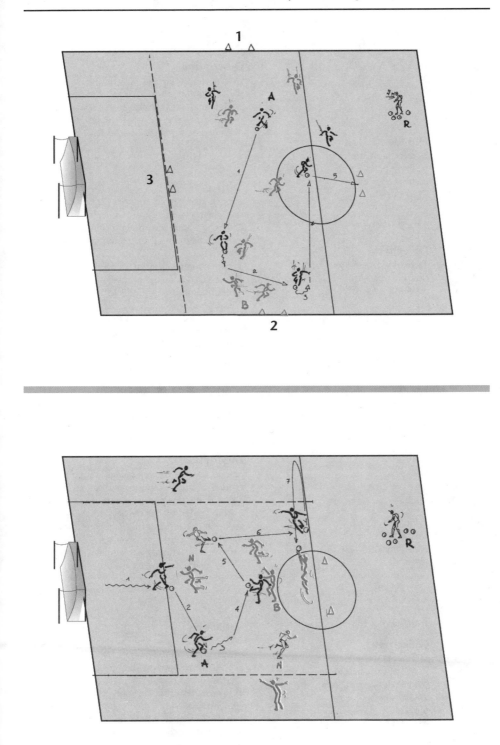

Exercise n. 80

Players
9.

Duration
20 minutes. Change of position between all players after every three minutes.

Objectives
Tactical play to improve first time passing 1-2 combinations, dribbling etc.

Description
On the 40 x 40 meter pitch divided into two parts, **1** and **2**, group 3A attacks the 5-meter goal defended by group 3B in under 1 minute. Immediately after group 3B attacks the goal defended by group 3C in area **2**.

Variations
1) Each group has a support player who acts as a playmaker.
2) The attacking group plays first time passes and the defending group plays without restrictions.
3) One player is designated to shoot.
4) If the defenders gain possession they have to maintain it for 1 minute with first time passing.
5) At R's signal the three groups join up to continue playing 5 attacking players against 4 defenders.

Exercise n. 81

Players
8 + 1 goalkeeper.

Duration
15/20 minutes.

Objectives
1) The players use the width of the pitch to pass each other the ball.
2) Contrast between two players for possession and fast organization of attack.

Description
The goalkeeper throws the ball to the two groups 4A and 4B on the small pitch. The group that gains possession has to attack the goal defended by the keeper and the other group in under 1 minute. If, during the attack, the defenders gain possession they take the ball over the hallway line and start the attack on the goal defended by the other group.

Variations
1) 5 against 5 + 2 support players who direct the play both in defense and in attack.
2) One group plays to keep possession and the other plays to attack the goal.
3) Restrict times for dribbling the ball and 1-2 combinations.
4) Attack on goal only from the wings.
5) Limited touches.

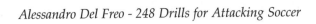

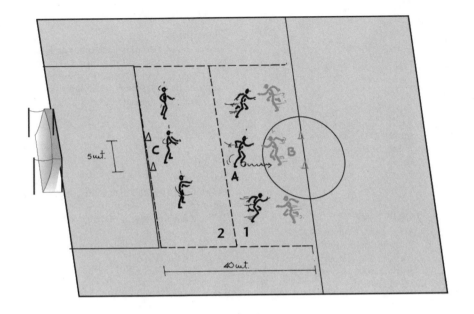

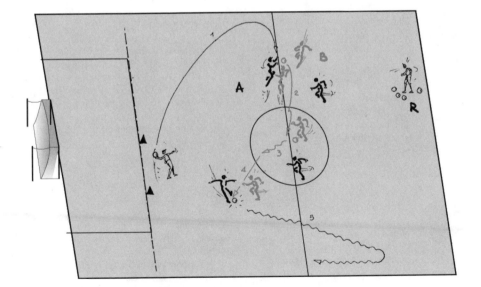

Exercise n. 82

Players
8 + 2 goalkeepers.

Duration
15/20 minutes. Every minute the group in possession has to finish.

Objectives
1) Fast attacking moves.
2) Continuous involve-ment of players off the field to assist in build-up to shots.

Description
Groups 2A and 2B play each other assisted by another 2A and 2B on the wings. Every minute the groups have to shoot at the mini-goals defended by the keepers. The players on the wings can pass to each other.

Variations
1) Groups 2A and 2B play with 2 support players.
2) The goalkeepers join in the attack with shots at goal.
3) The players on the wings switch with the players in the center.

Exercise n. 83

Players
16 + 2 goalkeepers.

Duration
15/20 minutes.
The players from each group switch positions every 5 minutes.

Objectives
Rationalization of indi-vidual actions and con-centration of tactical play for the team.

Description
Groups 3A and 3B play two-touch soccer in the penalty areas to attack the goals defended by the goalkeepers. At R's signal the group with the ball passes it to their teammate down the center of the field who moves into the oppo-nents' area to attack the regular goal. He is assisted by the players outside the area in his group. The goalkeeper and the other group defend the goal.

Variations
1) The four attacking players play first time passes and the three defenders use all combi-nations.
2) A support player on the wings who assists with first time passes.
3) Only shots from outside the box.

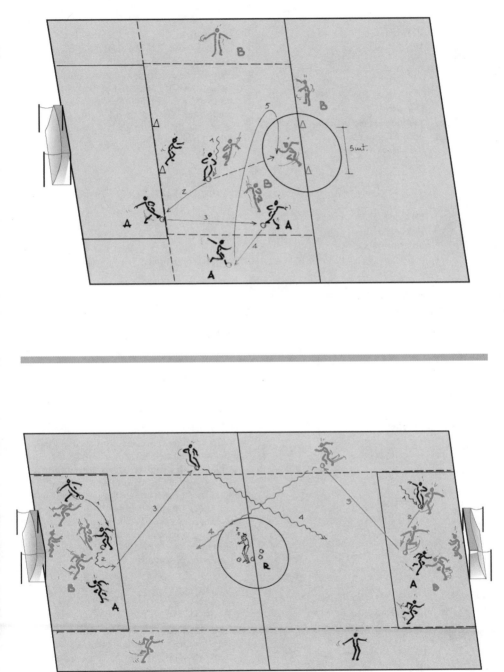

Exercise n. 84

Players
12 + 1 goalkeeper.

Duration
18/10 attacking moves on the regular goal (one every two minutes).

Objectives
Players' adaptation to offensive tactics.

Description
Groups 3A and 3B play each other in area **1**. Both groups dribble the ball. At R's signal the group in possession passes it to its teammates in area **2** who are defended by two of the other group and a third player who has come into play from off the goal line. The group with the ball attacks the regular goal and must finish in under thirty seconds.

Variations
1) 4 against 4 in area **1** and 3 against 3 in area **2**.
2) At R's signal the player with the ball moves into area **2** to play 3 against 2.
3) Limit the touches in area **1** and allow unlimited touches in area **2**.

Exercise n. 85

Players
9 + 1 support player + 1 goalkeeper.

Duration
15/20 minutes.

Objectives
1) Tactical play characterized by the flow of the attacking moves and defensive play and a constant rhythm in the move.
2) Improvement of precision of shots for technique.

Description
Group 5A moves forward from midfield to attack the goal defended by group 4B. Group 4A plays with two playmakers and group 4B with a sweeper. Once group A has passed the dotted line it passes the ball around and finishes in under 1 minute, with only the playmakers allowed to score. When group B gains possession it moves over the dotted line to switch roles with group A and the support player becomes its playmaker.

Variations
1) The playmakers shoot from a distance.
2) At R's signal the roles are quickly inverted.
3) The defenders slow down the pace to prevent fast attacking moves.

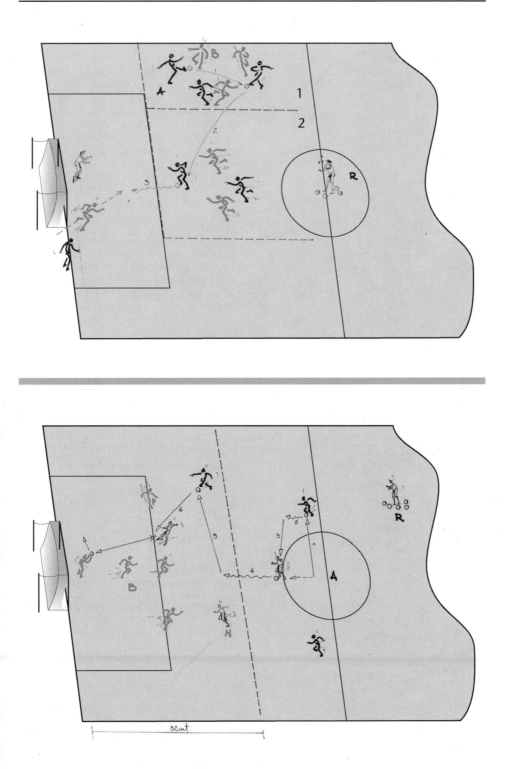

Exercise n. 86

Players
14 + 1 support player
+ 2 goalkeepers.

Duration
20/30 minutes.

Description
Group 4A plays group 4B in midfield. Group 4B is restricted to 3 touches and assisted by a support player. At R's signal the group in possession attacks the goal in area **2** defended by group C. If group C gains possession it attacks the goal in area **1** which is defended by the group which had not attacked. The two players off the field come in to play with the group which is starting the counter-attack.

Objectives
Build-up of the break on both sides of the field.

Variations
1) Three first time passes and shot at goal.
2) Only the support player shoots at goal.
3) At R's signal the groups from area **1** join each other to attack the goal defended by group C in area **2**. 8 against 4 + 1 support player.

Exercise n. 87

Players
8 + 3 support players.

Duration
Five 5 minute sessions.

Description
Groups 4A and4B play each other with a support player on a small pitch. Both groups play three touches substitute the support player in play.

Variations
1) The support player must assist play with long passes.
2) Play concentrated on dribbling the ball.

Objectives
Tactical move to facilitate substitution of players and improve play.

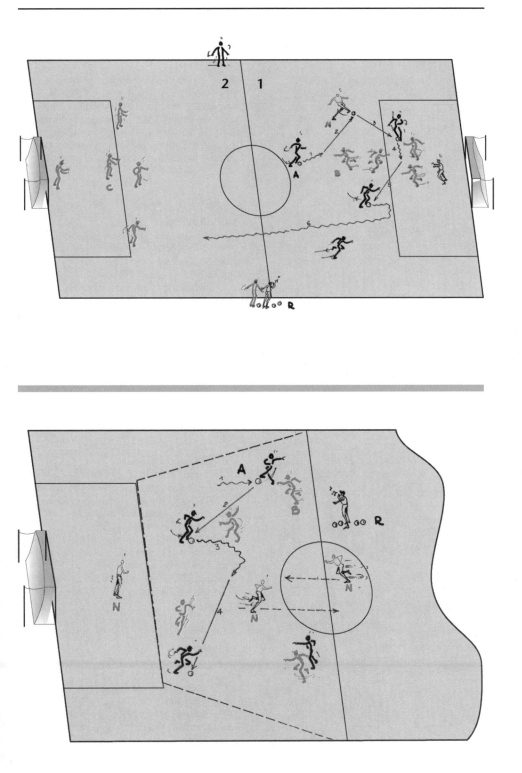

Exercise n. 88

Players
6 + 1 goalkeeper.

Duration
15 minutes. Change of positions of groups every 3 minutes.

Objectives
1) Tactical play to improve vision on the field.
2) Move with a playmaker to improve dribbling and 1-2 combinations.
3) Run into position of playmaker followed by a finishing shot.

Description
Group 3A plays two-touch soccer to attack the goal defended by group 3B and the goalkeeper on a small pitch. The players of team A play first time passes, 1-2 combinations and dribble the ball. The shots are taken by the playmaker. If group B gains possession it passes the ball to group C in midfield to substitute group A.

Variations
1) Playmaker takes shot form outside the box.
2) If group 3B gains possession they start to attack assisted by group 1A.
3) Shot only from inside the area.
4) The attacking group must touch the ball at least five times before shooting.
5) First time shot.

Exercise n. 89

Players
7 + 2 support players + 1 goalkeeper.

Duration
Five 5 minute session.

Objectives
Series of individual and team moves for basic tactics.

Description
On the small pitch group 4A defends the goal with the goalkeeper while group 3B defends the 10-meter goal with two support players. A player from group A must dribble the ball across one of the small goals in under 1 minute. If group 3B gains possession with the help of the two support players it attacks the regular goal playing two touches and has to score in under 30 seconds. All the players of each team have to touch the ball before finishing.

Variations
1) Two players of group A play two touches and two play first time touches.
2) Only one designated player from 3B is allowed to shoot.
3) The support player who gains possession moves forward and acts as a playmaker for group B.

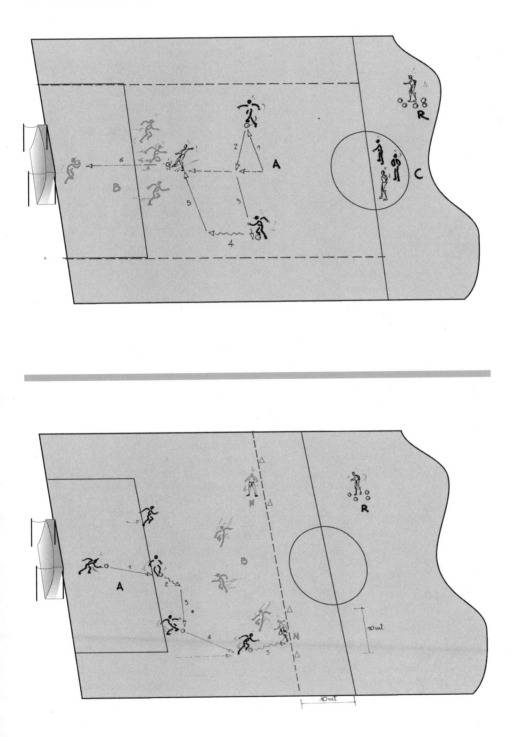

Exercise n. 90

Players
12.

Duration
Six 3 minute sessions.

Objectives
1) Keeping play moving with involvement of players in all areas.
2) Co-ordination of move through fast, flowing passes.

Description
Groups 6A and 6B play each other on a small pitch. Each group has 2 players who play inside the areas indicated with the dotted lines. When one of these gains possession he moves out of the area dribbling the ball and is substituted by another player of the same group.

Variations
1) One group plays to keep possession and the other to attack.
2) 5 against 4. Both groups dribble the ball.
3) Each group has a playmaker.

Exercise n. 91

Players
18 + 2 support players + 2 goalkeepers.

Duration
Five 5 minute sessions.

Objectives
1) Tactical move for fast attacking play.
2) Perfection of dribbling of the ball and speed of shot.

Description
Two groups, 9A and 9B play each other on a regular pitch. One of the players of the group in possession of the ball has to enter a 10 x 10 meter area with the ball. This area is defended by a player from the other group. The player from the attacking group has to dribble past his opponent. The support players assist the play with long passes. Every 2 minutes the group in possession of the ball has to enter the indicated areas.

Variations
1) The attacking players are substituted by support players.
2) The support players act as playmakers.
3) Shots from outside the area.

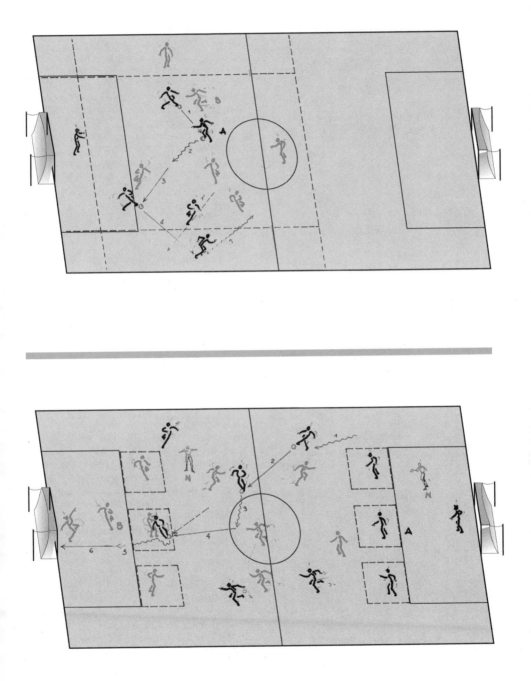

Exercise n. 92

Players
4 + 4 goalkeepers.

Duration
20 minutes. The players change positions every 5 minutes.

Objectives
Tactical phase to improve vision in attack.

Description
Groups 2A and 2B play each other in areas **1** and **2**. When group 2B goes over the dotted line in the center of the field with the ball group 2A comes off the goal line to the pitch to defend the goal. The two goalkeepers only use their feet and play in defense as well. When the two defenders gain possession they attack the goal in the opposite area. Once they go past the dotted line in the center of the field they are attacked by two defenders of another group. The attacking group must finish in under 1 minute.

Variations
1) A support player comes onto the pitch with the two defenders.
2) Each group has a player designated to take shots.
3) When the defenders gain possession they must attack the opponents' goal in under 30 seconds.

Exercise n. 93

Players
4 + 1 support player + 1 goalkeeper.

Duration
15 minutes.

Objectives
1) The two groups look for the support player who acts as a playmaker outside the penalty area and provides passes for the attack.
2) The player in possession of the ball has to free his teammate to finish.

Description
On a small pitch the goalkeeper throws the ball to the support player who is waiting outside the penalty area. The support player feeds the ball to group 2A in the area who attack the goal defended by the goalkeeper and group 2B. Group 2A dribbles the ball only. If the defenders gain possession during the attacking move they pass the ball to the support player who returns it for 2B to attack and 2A to defend.

Variations
1) A support player along the edges of the box who takes angled shots at goal.
2) 3 against 3 + 1 support player in the penalty area who plays with the group that doesn't have possession.
3) Shot after 1-2 combination.

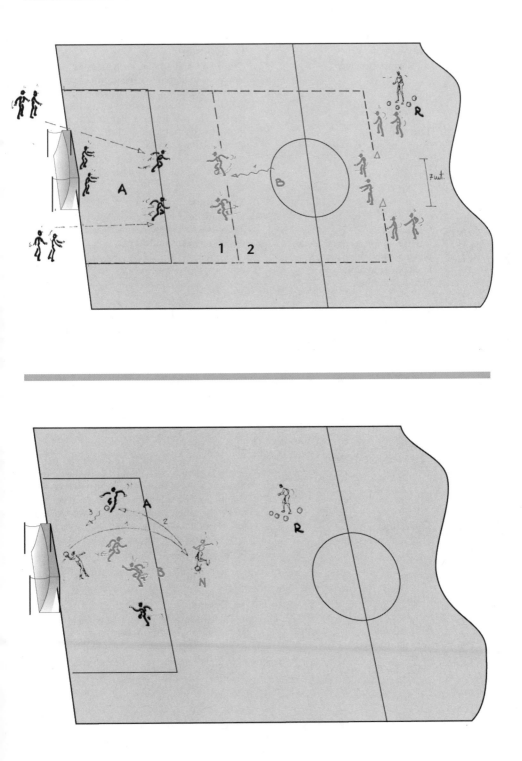

Exercise n. 94

Players
8 + 2 support players.

Duration
Four 5 minute sessions.

Objectives
Intensify movement of players with long balls from one side of the field to the other.

Description
Groups 4A and 4B play each other for possession on a small pitch. Each group plays two touches. A player from each group plays inside a 15 x 20 meter area to supply fast, first time passes. The two support players play with the group in possession of the ball and assist the play with long passes.

Variations
1) Limited touches for the support players.
2) The player inside the area marked with the dotted line joins in the attack.

Exercise n. 95

Players
12 + 2 support players.

Duration
Six 5 minute sessions.

Objectives
Alternate between attacking and defensive moves for the improvement of specific individual characteristics.

Description
Group 3A plays group 3B and group 3C plays group 3D in the areas marked with the dotted lines. At a signal from R the group in possession passes the ball to the support player inside the center circle in midfield who kicks it into the other area. The group that gains possession attacks the regular goal defended by the other group.

Variations
1) The two support players play inside the areas indicated by the dotted lines.
2) The support player moves into the indicated area with the ball.
3) The ball is to be dribbled only.

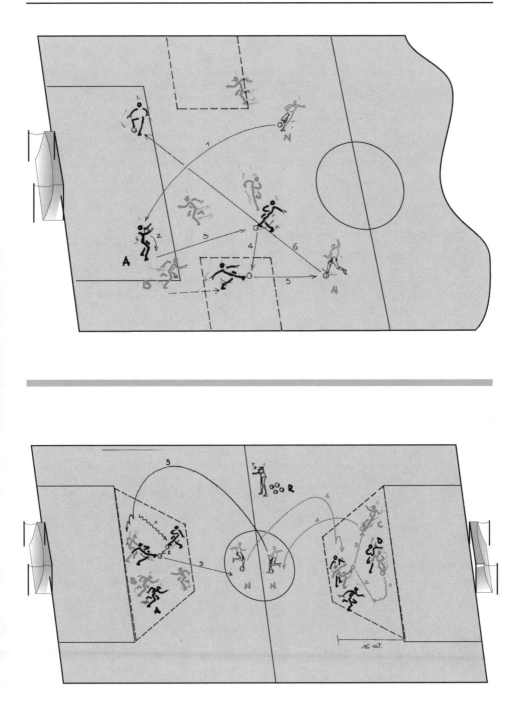

Exercise n. 96

Players
8 + 2 support players.

Duration
10/12 moves. Change of positions every 2 minutes.

Objectives
1) Tactical build-up for intensive play.
2) Changes of position and play for rapid adaptation to varying situations.

Description
Groups 2A and 2B play each other in midfield. When the group with the ball passes the line going from one area to the other, 1 and 2, 4 players enter the field. Two players join each group and the attacking moves have to be finished in under 1 minute. If the defending group gains possession it attacks the goal defended by the other group. They play 4 against 4 to finish in under 1 minute. The play continues 2A against 2B and so on.

Variations
1) The two players who have come into play cannot play the ball to each other.
2) The game starts 2A against 4B to finish 6B against 4A.
3) Limited touches once the players go over the dotted line.
4) The teams change position once every move has been concluded (the external players become attacking players etc.)

Exercise n. 97

Players
10 + 2 support players + 2 goalkeepers.

Duration
15/20 minutes. Change of positions every 5 minutes.

Objectives
Shift the play from one side of the pitch to the other before shooting at goal.

Description
Groups 4A and 4B play two-touch soccer to shoot at goal. Each group builds up its attack by kicking the ball over a 20-meter space in the center of the pitch. Each group has one of its players in the right hand zone of attack of the opponents' area. This player plays first time passes and can only be tackled by one member of the opposing team. The two support players play in the right hand zones of defense and assist the play with long, precise passes.

Variations
1) The player in the right hand zone can move out but he must be substituted immediately by another player from the same group.
2) The support players can move out but they must shoot as quickly as possible.
3) One group plays to keep possession, the other to attack both goals.
4) A 10-meter space in the center.

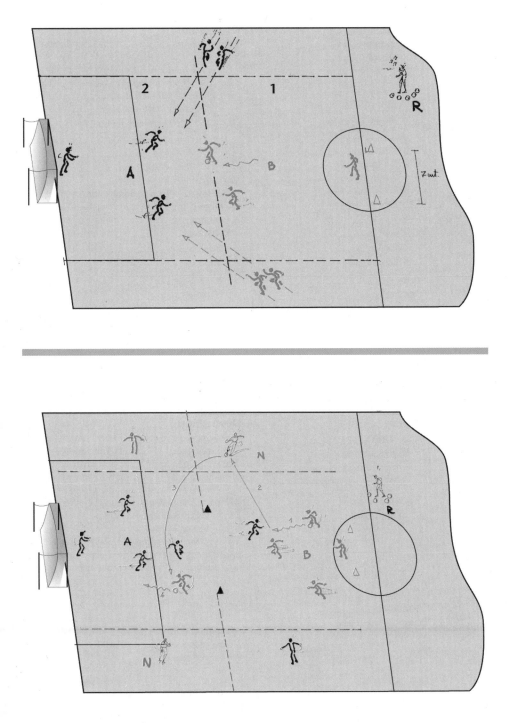

Exercise n. 98

Players
16 + 2 support players + 2 goalkeepers.

Duration
Six 5 minute sessions.

Description
4 defenders play against 4 attacking players in each half of the field, **1** and **2**. At R's signal the teams play a long ball from one half to the other. The group that gains possession attacks the goal in its own half defended by the other team. The support player plays with the team in possession and acts as a playmaker.

Objectives
Wide vision of play and co-operation between teammates.

Variations
1) One team plays various combinations and the other is limited to three touches.
2) One group is restricted to playing inside the penalty area.

Exercise n. 99

Players
16 + 2 support players + 2 goalkeepers.

Duration
25/30 minutes non-stop play.

Description
Each team has an area 40 meters long where 4A plays against 4B. In area **1** the goalkeeper throws the ball to the support player who plays it on to the player on the same team in the other area. In each area the group in possession of the ball attacks and the other defends. If the defenders gain possession the support player passes it to the attacking teammates in the other area. No player must enter the 30-meter area in midfield. Every two minutes the team in possession must shoot.

Objectives
Tactics for team play and efficiency of players.

Variations
1) The support player can enter the central area of the field with the ball.
2) The defenders keep the ball for two minutes with rapid passes.

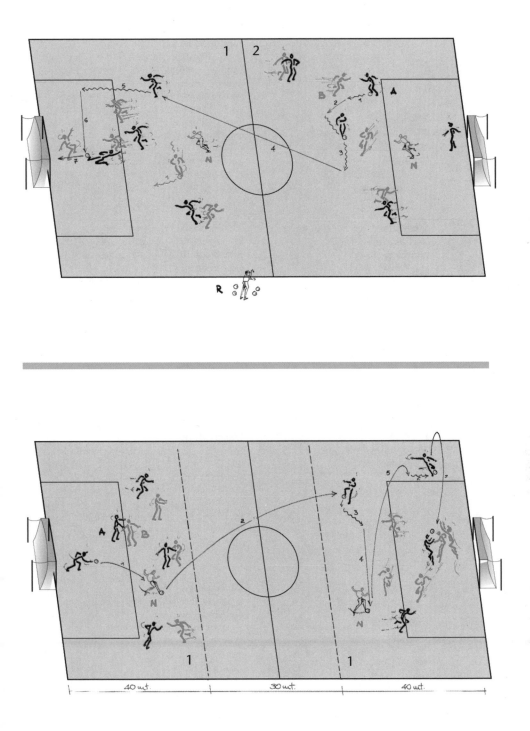

Exercise n. 100

Players
12 + 2 support players.

Duration
15/20 minutes. Players change positions every 5 minutes.

Objectives
1) Lateral moves of the attacking players to shoot at the small goals.
2) Defensive tactics for pressure play.

Description
In area **1** group 3A defends the two mini goals from group 3B in attack. In area **2** group 3B defends the mini goals from group 3A. Two support players play each other in the central area. The game starts from the defenders in area **1** who pass to a support player in the central area to play it on to the attacking players in area **2** to finish in the mini-goals. The move has to be finished in under 1 minute. After each move R starts the play from the opposing area.

Variations
1) The attacking group has a player who dribbles the ball while the other two play 1-2 combinations.
2) The defenders play with one of their team-mates as a goalkeeper and the others confront the attacking players.

Example n. 101

Players
10 + 2 support player + 2 goalkeepers.

Duration
3/4 five minute sessions

Objectives
1) Fast exchanges of the ball with changes of position and play.
2) Movement of the play to the wings.

Description
Group 5A plays group 5B on a small pitch. A player from each team plays 1-2 combinations and first time passes from the wings. If he moves out in possession of the ball he is immediately replaced by another player from the same group. The support player acts as a playmaker for both attacking moves and in defense.

Variations
1) 6 against 6 + 2 support players who only play first time passes.
2) Shots only from the wings.
3) Only headers to finish.

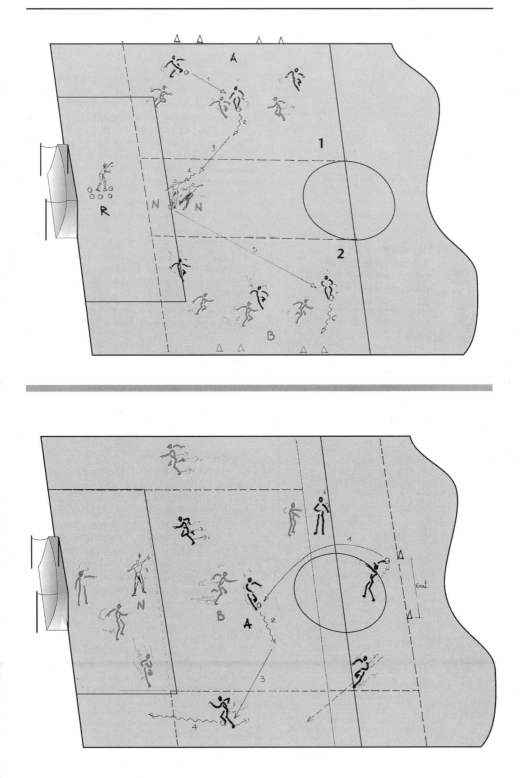
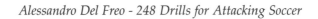

Exercise n. 102

Players
6.

Duration
3/5 five minute sessions. All players change positions every 3 minutes.

Objectives
Perfection of technique and tactics through flow of the move.

Description
Groups 2A and 2B play each other for possession on a small pitch. One of the players in group 2A plays three-touch soccer while the other plays all combinations. One of the players in group 2B plays two-touch soccer while the other dribbles the ball. At R's signal one of the groups moves out of the area to be immediately substituted by another group. Play must not be interrupted during the substitution of the groups.

Variations
1) 2 against 2 + 1 support player who assists first-time passes and 1-2 combinations.
2) Finishing in the small goals only dribbling the ball.
3) At R's signal a player leaves the field and play continues 2 against 1.

Exercise n. 103

Players
14 + 2 support players + 2 goalkeepers.

Duration
25'/30' minutes. All players change positions every 5 minutes.

Objectives
Movement of play to the wings with long passes.

Description
Groups 7A and 7B play each other for possession and have to play a shot in under two minutes. One of the groups attacks moving across the dotted lines on the edges of the pitch. Only two players can move into these areas, one for each team. The player in the area must dribble the ball and play long high crosses. The two support players play as playmakers both in attacking moves and in defense. They dribble the ball, play first time passes and 1-2 combinations.

Variations
1) 5 against 5. All players play three-touch soccer.
2) The support players play long passes.
3) Only the support players shoot from outside the area.

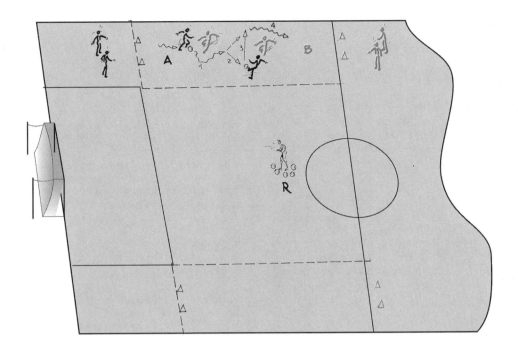

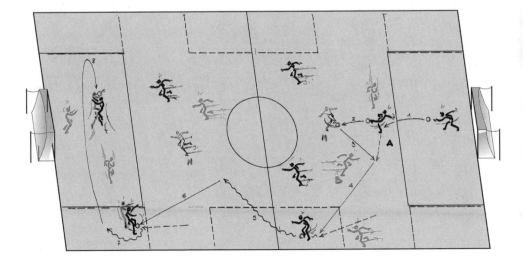

Exercise n. 104

Players
14 + 3 support players + 2 goalkeepers.

Duration
15/20 minutes. Every three minutes the players change area and position.

Objectives
1) Fast vision of play.
2) Free the ball rapidly.
3) Tactics for build-up of rapid move.

Description
Groups 2A and 2B play each other for possession in area **1**. The group in possession passes the ball to its teammates in area **2** over a 15 meter area. In area **2** group 3A plays group 3B, they can play up to three touches and pass the ball to their teammates across a fifteen meter area. In area **3** groups 2A and 2B play for possession. A support player plays in each area as a playmaker. If a group loses possession the other group attacks in the opposite direction. When area **1** is without a ball R throws another into play to keep the game moving.

Variations
1) 10 against 9 + 2 support players.
2) In area **2** only first time passes are to be played.
3) The player with the ball in area **2** can move into area **3** to play 3 against 2.
4) At R's signal the players in area **2** pass the ball back to area **1** for the finish.

Exercise n. 105

Players
10 + 2 goalkeepers.

Duration
Six 5 minute sessions.

Objectives
The group in possession uses the wing for one player who has to move out rapidly to keep the pace moving.

Description
Groups 5A and 5B play two-touch soccer on a small pitch. Only one player from each team can enter the lateral areas of the pitch to free himself of his opponent and to dribble the ball to create a fast finish. The group in possession of the ball must move into the lateral area at least once before finishing.

Variations
1) Two support players on the wings for the shots at goal.
2) Only vertical shots at goal.

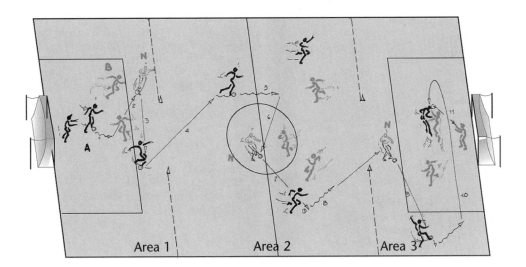

Exercise n. 106

Players
20 + 2 support players.

Duration
5/6 five minute session.

Objectives
1) Move involving first time passes, short balls and 1-2 combinations.
2) Adaptation of players to defensive and offensive tactics.

Description
Groups 5A and 5B play on a small pitch. They pass the ball across the small 3-meter goal. The support player assists fast passes. At the same time in area **2** the players pass the ball after the player has gone through the small goal with the ball.

Variations
1) 6 against 4 + 4 support players.
2) At R's signal the player with the ball shoots at the regular goal.

Exercise n. 107

Players
10 + 2 support players.

Duration
20 minutes. Every 5 minutes all players change positions.

Objectives
1) Tactical move for improvement of fast, incisive attacking moves.
2) Development of difficult technical and tactical play in defensive and offensive roles.

Description
Groups 5A and 5B play each other to finish. Group 5A attacks the regular goal with diagonal crosses and group 5B dribbles the ball and plays 1-2 combinations to finish in the goal in midfield. At R's signal the two groups pass the ball to the support player and move to a goal indicated by R to receive a corner (group A continues to attack and group B continues to defend). The corners from T and Z are alternated by R after every three minutes of play. After the corner kick the groups receive the ball from a neutral player to continue attacking the two goals.

Variations
1) One group attacks with vertical crosses and the other plays diagonal crosses.
2) After the corner kick a defender and an attacking player switch groups.

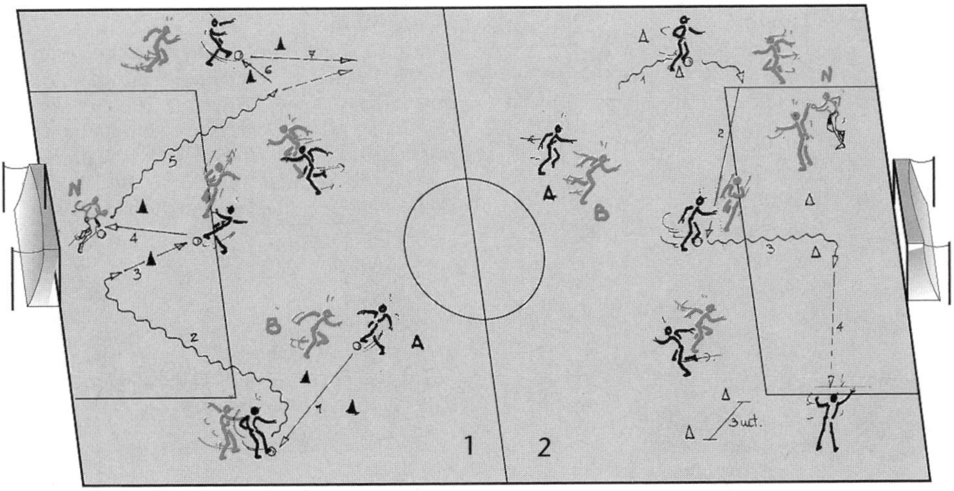
N
B
A
1
2
A
B
N
3 yd.

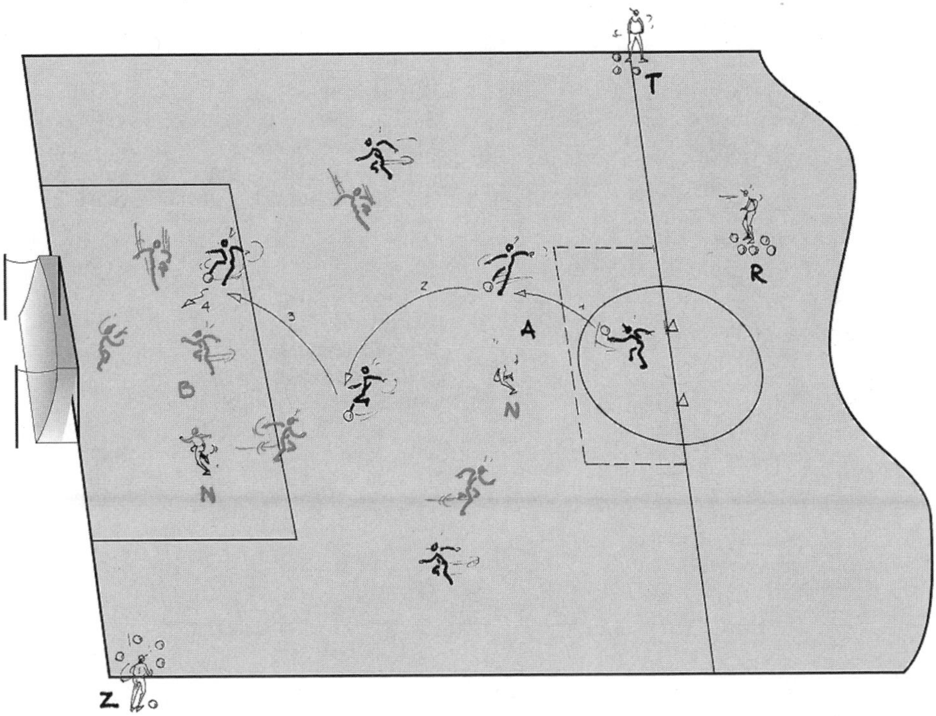
T
R
A
B
N
N
Z

Exercise n. 108

Players
15 + 1 goalkeeper.

Duration
Two 10 minute sessions.

Objectives
1) Movement of two players with the ball.
2) Precision of technique despite the reduced number of defenders.

Description
Group 5A attacks the goal defended by group 4B. The game ends when the attacking team misses the shot and the defense gains possession. At R's signal a player from group B (the fifth) comes on to defend the goal. The finishing must be concluded inside the area. Group C enters the area to alternate with group A.

Variations
1) Play on the wings.
2) The defenders are outside the area.
3) Shots from outside the area.

Exercise n. 109

Players
15 + 2 goalkeepers.

Duration
Four 8 minute sessions.

Objectives
1) Mainly attacking play.
2) Move play to the wings to build-up the attack.

Description
Group 5A attacks the goal defended by group 5B in under 30 seconds. If group A loses the ball or score, play continues with group B attacking in area **2** defended by group 5C.

Variations
1) Limited touches.
2) Small pitch with 7 against 7.
3) Introduce 2 support players.

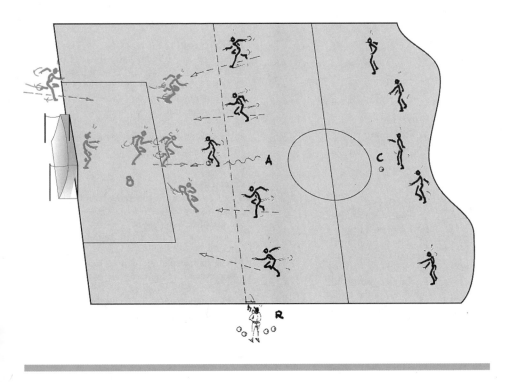

Exercise n. 110

Players
10.

Duration
4/5 five minute sessions.

Objectives
1) Tactical play to create new moves through displacement of groups from one playing area to another.
2) The two groups use the space of the two areas of play to move the ball around and keep the game moving.

Description
Groups 5A and 5B play each other for possession to attack goals C and D on the small pitch **1**. At R's signal the groups take the play into area **2** to attack the goals M and N with three-touch soccer and 1-2 combinations. In area **1** the groups attack the goals C and D with vertical passes whereas when they move into area **2** they attack goals M and N and play diagonal balls to each other.

Variations
1) All players must touch the ball before the finishing shot.
2) Shot after two passes.
3) 5 against 5 in area **1** and 7 against 7 in area **2**.
4) The groups playing in area **1** only shoot when they enter the last rectangle of the pitch.
5) In area **1** one group plays to maintain possession and the other to shoot. In area **2** the groups switch positions.
6) 5 against 5 + 1 support player. At R's signal the support player switches the play to areas **1** and **2**.

Exercise n. 111

Players
20 + 2 goalkeepers.

Duration
Five 5 minute sessions.

Description
Group 3B plays three-touch soccer to attack the goal defended by the goalkeeper and group 3A in area **1**. In areas **2** and **3** groups 2A and 2B play for possession. In area **4** group 3A attacks the goal defended by the goalkeeper and group 3B which plays three-touch soccer.

Objectives
Improvement of the game through fast passing and attacking moves and defense.

Variations
1) In areas **1** and **4** the attacking move must be finished in under 1 minute.
2) Alternate the roles of attacking players and defenders in areas **1** and **4**.
3) Two supportive players in areas **2** and **3** who move the ball from one area to another.
4) Play mainly first time passes and 1-2 combinations.

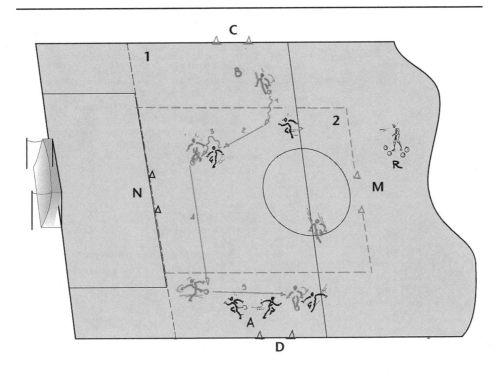

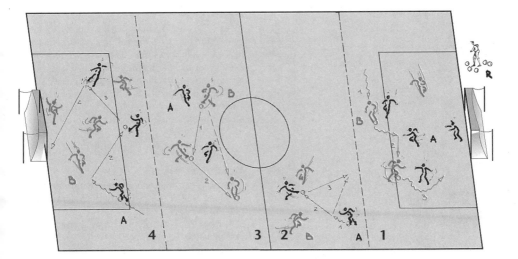

Exercise n. 112

Players
14 + 3 support players.

Duration
Four 5 minute sessions.

Description
Groups 4A and 4B play in area **1**. At R's signal the group in possession passes the ball into area **2** to the support player who plays it on to the player of the same group in area **3**. He must finish in under 30 seconds while the other group defends. Groups 3A and 3B play in area **3**.

Objectives
1) Movement of players and the ball.
2) The support player intensifies the play.

Variations
1) The support player enters area **2** with the ball.
2) Players dribble the ball in area **1**.
3) R signals the change of play regularly.
4) 5 against 5.
5) At R's signal a player from area **1** takes the ball into area **3**.

Exercise n. 113

Players
20 + 2 goalkeepers.

Duration
15 minutes.

Description
In area **1** groups 4A and 4B play each other for possession and pass the ball to their teammates in areas **2** and **3** in under 20 seconds. Group A passes to attacking teammates in area **2** and group B to its attacking teammates in area **3**. In areas **2** and **3**, three attacking players of one group play against three defenders of the other. The attacking move must be finished in under 30 seconds.

Objectives
Tactical adaptation of the players to develop attacking and defensive moves.

Variations
1) A player from area **1** can move into the attackers area of the field with the ball and play 4 against 3.
2) A support player plays in areas **2** and **3** exclusively to shoot at goal.
3) When group A moves from area **1** into area **2**, at R's signal group B moves into area **3** from area **1** to attack.

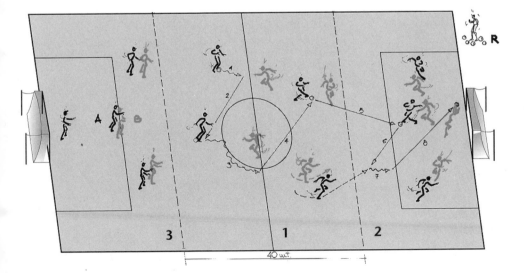

CHAPTER THREE

Tactical development for the creation of new solutions in attack

1) Effective position of the players on the pitch.
2) Exercises with small goals on large playing areas.

In these exercises the player is confronted with elaborate technical moves which require a greatly modified tactical approach compared to the regular moves.

These technical procedures provide the basis on which tactical strategies for the team game can be built.

The player is forced to time his move well in order to co-ordinate with his teammates and regulate the conditions of speed and power in his execution of the move. This is a particularly important series of exercises for the co-ordinated movements of the players who develop their physical and mental ability through elaborate maneuvers.

Exercise n. 114

Players
12 + 2 support players + 2 goalkeepers.

Duration
15'-20'.

Objectives
Possession of the ball for the build-up of tactical play and concentration of team play.

Description
The goalkeeper plays a long ball to the support player who is in a 10 x 10 meter area just beyond the halfway line. The support player controls the ball and quickly plays it on into the opposite penalty area to groups 3A and 3B. The group that wins possession attacks the goal which is defended by the goalkeeper and the other group without moving out of the penalty area. At the same time the game is played in the other direction with another support player.

Variations
1) One player is designated to shoot.
2) The support player moves out of the 10 x 10 meter area to carry the ball into the penalty area to play with the group chosen by R.
3) 2 against 2 in the area or 6 against 4.

Exercise n. 115

Players
6 + 2 support players + 1 goalkeeper.

Duration
15/20 minutes. R speeds up the play by changing the attack every two minutes.

Objectives
Combination of individual skills and team play for basic tactics.

Description
In the small area group 3A plays group 3B for possession. Group 3B plays three-touch soccer. At R's signal the two groups move rapidly into the penalty area to receive two balls from the support players in the corners. The two balls are played in succession. Group A plays headers, rapid passes and shots from the crosses while group B defends.

Variations
1) One of the attacking players stops on the edge of the box to receive the cross and start the build-up to the attack.
2) If the defenders gain possession the position of the two groups are inverted.
3) The support players cross from the corners in quick succession.

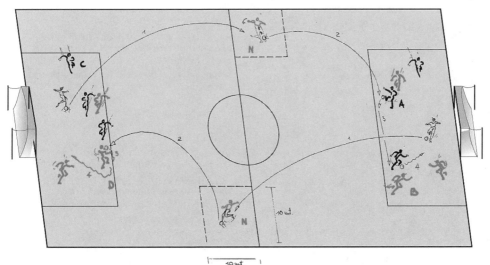

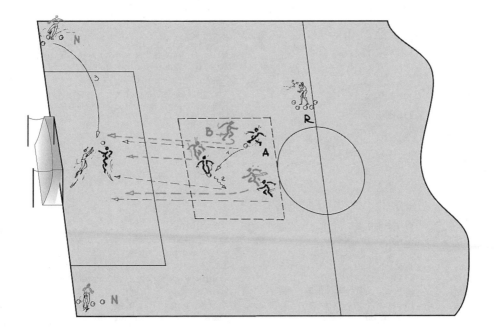

Exercise n. 116

Players
10 + 2 support players + 2 goalkeepers.

Duration
20'.

Objectives
1) Attacking move in both directions without one team interfering with the play of the other.
2) Technical and tactical move for fast diagonal first time passes and long, high crosses for conclusive headers.

Description
Group 5A plays first time passes to attack the goal defended by the goalkeeper and a support player who comes into play from off the field to tackle the attacking player who heads at goal. The move is to be finished in under 20 seconds. Group B attacks the other goal at the same time.

Variations
1) The goalkeepers start the move by throwing the ball long and high into the opposite field.
2) 3 support players come into play from off the field to take possession and attack the goal which is defended by the four players.

Exercise n. 117

Players
7 + 1 goalkeepers.

Duration
25/30 throws from R.
After 5 throws all players change positions.

Objectives
1) Concentration of groups A and C on the ball.
2) Group 2C uses the entire area to pass, dribble and play 1-2 combinations before the final shot.

Description
From R's long throw B, who is inside area **1**, takes the ball down and plays a high cross into the box for group 2C who plays a rapid shot. The goal is defended by group 3A. R kicks the ball into area **2** in moderate succession to repeat the exercise.

Variations
1) The player in possession from group C is put under pressure by the players from group 3A.
2) After each shot at goal an attacking player switches with a defender.
3) A support player plays with group A to maintain possession and with group B only to shoot at goal.

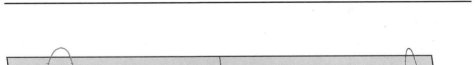

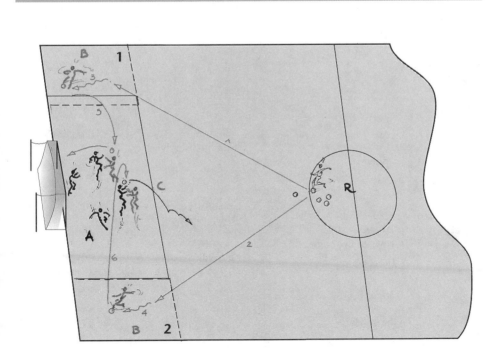

Exercise n. 118

Players
16.

Duration
15/20 minutes. The group alternates attacking players with defenders every 5 minutes.

Objectives
Tactical play for the build-up of attacking moves and defensive play through improvement of technique of dribbling, 1-2's and first time passes.

Description
Group A plays with three defenders and 2 goalkeepers in area **1**. The keepers can only use their feet. In the same area the goal is attacked by group B with two players standing at the corners and a third player who moves around the pitch. In area **2** the groups A and B switch roles. The move is built up in under 1 minute with the defenders feeding the ball from one area to the attacking players of the same group in the other area. If the opponents gain possession they move play into the other area with their own attacking group who finish. No player can move into the central area indicated by the dotted lines.

Variations
1) All defenders must touch the ball before playing it to their attacking players.
2) A defender can cross the central area and play 4 against 3 in the opponents' area.

Exercise n. 119

Players
11 + 2 goalkeeper.

Duration
15/20 minutes.

Objectives
1) The two groups have to use the entire field dribbling the ball to build up the move.
2) Attacking move from the wings and finish from the center.

Description
Group 5B attacks the goal defended by group 6A on the small pitch. The player in possession from group B builds up the attacking move across a 15-meter area on the wings with rapid passes and applies pressure to the attacking team to defend the goal.

Variations
1) The attacking group has to play a 1-2 combination after crossing the 15-meter area before shooting.
2) At R's signal two players switch positions.
3) 6 attacking players against 4 defenders.

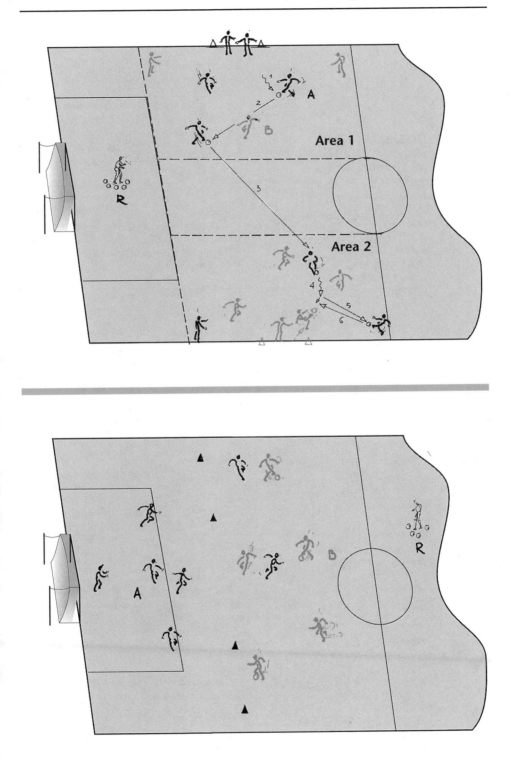

Exercise n. 120

Players
11 + 1 goalkeeper.

Duration
15 minutes. The groups change positions every three minutes.

Objectives
1) Movement of players and ball for incisive attacking moves.
2) Important for group B to move the attacking play from one side of the field to the other.

Description
Group 5B attacks the goal defended by the goalkeeper and group 6A in midfield. Group 6A plays two-touch soccer. Group B must move into one of the areas on the sides of the penalty area before shooting. The attacking players must dribble the ball only in these areas. Each attacking move must be concluded in under 1 minute.

Variations
1) When the defenders gain possession they must keep it for one minute.
2) 5 against 5 + 2 support players.
3) Finishing shot in under 30 seconds.

Exercise n. 121

Players
10 + 1 support player + 2 goalkeepers.

Duration
15 minutes. Every three minutes the players from each group switch position.

Objectives
1) Tactical move around the support player who directs the play with precise passes to the wings.
2) Tactical phase to improve vision on the field.

Description
Group 5A and 5B play for possession in area **1**. The support player assists the player and moves the play towards the wings with precise passes. The attacking group must finish with diagonal shots from the wings only.

Variations
1) The two attacking players on the wings pass the ball to each other before the finishing shot from the central area.
2) Build-up of the attacking move with two players on the wings, two in midfield and the fifth player who moves to hit the finishing shot.
3) The attacking player hits a left foot shot from the left wing and a right foot shot from the right wing.

Area 1

Exercise n. 122

Players
8 + 1 goalkeeper.

Duration
15 minutes. Change of position every three minutes.

Objectives
Specific move to improve players' skill in attacking moves.

Description
Group 4A attacks the goal defended by the goalkeeper and group 2B in midfield. Group 4A plays 1-2 combinations. The move is to finish with a header from inside the penalty area by a previously designated player. When the cross comes in from the wing for the conclusive header another player moves into play from off the field to assist the defense.

Variations
1) First time shot.
2) When the defenders gain possession they attack the goal from the wings. The goal is defended by the other group.
3) When the defenders gain possession two of them shoot from a distance and the other two dribble inside the box to shoot.

Exercise n. 123

Players
10 + 2 goalkeepers.

Duration
Three 8 minute sessions.

Objectives
1) Tactical play to improve vision on the field.
2) Mobility of players to organize fast moves on the field.

Description
Groups 5A and 5B play each other for possession on the small pitch. Both groups play two-touch soccer. The two groups play very short, diagonal passes to keep the play moving quickly. At R's signal a player from one group moves to the other to continue the play 6 against 4. All the players from one group must touch the ball before the final shot. Each group moves with the ball with three players at the center of the pitch, two of whom act as playmakers. The other two move along the wings to hit diagonal shots from the wings.

Variations
1) One player is designated for each group to take the shots.
2) At R's signal the group in possession passes the ball to the other group.
3) 5 against 5 plus 2 support players who only shoot at goal.

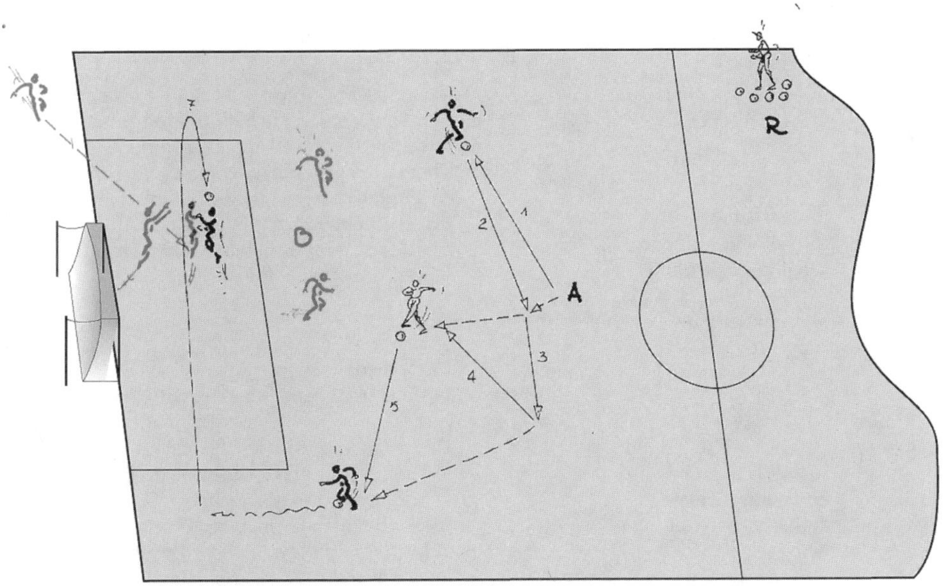
7
1
2
3
4
5
A
B
R

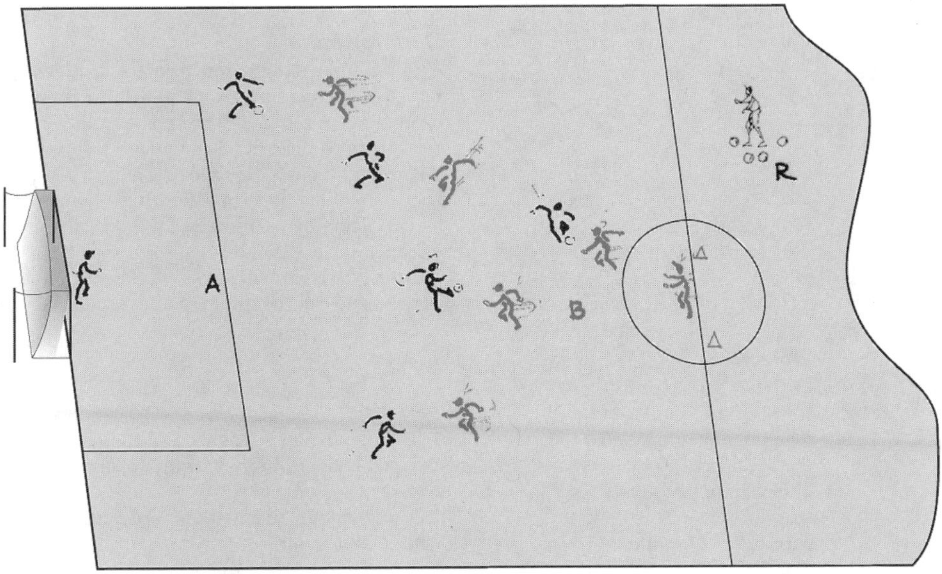
A
B
R

Exercise n. 124

Players
10 + 1 support players + 2 goalkeepers.

Duration
4/5 six minute sessions. Change of positions between attacking players and defenders every 6 minutes.

Objectives
1) The objective of the attack is to go beyond the neutral area and build up play on the wings.
2) Tactical play based on the rapid change from attack to defense and vice versa.

Description
Group 5A and 5B play each other for possession on the small pitch. Both groups play three-touch soccer. No player in possession from either group may enter into the 10-meter area in the center of the field. Only the support player can build up the move both in defense and attack from this area. All players must shoot from outside the area.

Variations
1) Shots from inside the box with first time passes.
2) The defense dribbles the ball only.
3) The support player dribbles the ball only.
4) The support player dribbles the ball out of the central area to finish from near the goals.
5) Each group plays with two playmakers who must not shoot.

Exercise n. 125

Players
10 + 1 goalkeeper.

Duration
15 minutes. Change of positions every three minutes.

Objectives
1) The attacking group moves the game around the playmaker to create the build-up.
2) Finishing inside certain times that must not exceed the 2 minute mark.

Description
Group 5A plays three -touch soccer to attack the goal defended by group 5B. All the players form group A must play fast passes and 1-2 combinations to each other. One player from the group acts as a playmaker. The attack builds up along the wings which are defended by two defenders. Group B plays with a sweeper. If the defenders gain possession the roles are changed with group A. The playmaker remains with the group in attack.

Variations
1) The playmaker heads the ball to finish.
2) The defender interferes with the attack slowing down the play.
3) 5 attacking players with two playmakers who do not shoot.
4) Limited touches of the ball.
5) At R's signal the roles of the two groups are inverted.

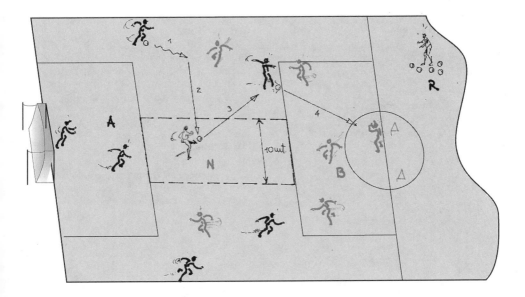

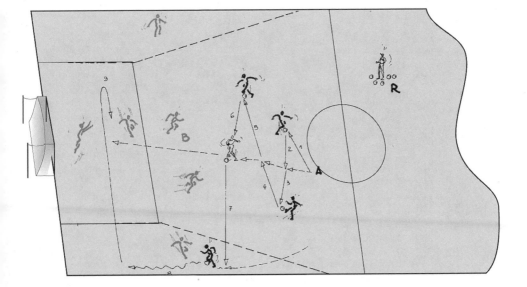

Exercise n. 126

Players
8 + 1 goalkeeper.

Duration
15/20 sessions. A shot must be taken every minute and the players must change position every three minutes.

Objectives
Vision on the pitch with the play kept moving and players alternating with each other at R's signal.

Description
The midfield is divided into areas **1** and **2**, group 5A plays two-touch soccer and attacks the goal in area **2** which is defended by the goalkeeper and group 3B. The attacking team must finish with a header.

Variations
1) Header from a designated player.
2) When the attacking move goes past the line marked in the center of the field one of the players moves into a defensive position.
3) When the defenders gain possession they dribble the ball over the dotted line in mid-field.

Exercise n. 127

Players
8 + 2 support players.

Duration
4/5 five minute sessions. Players change position every 5 minutes.

Objectives
1) Quick changes of position through move-ment of players and the ball.
2) Tactical play to keep players dribbling the ball.

Description
Groups 4A and 3B play each other for posses-sion to attack the 5-meter goal on the small pitch. Each group has a player on the right wing of the attack. He assists 1-2 combinations and long crosses. He can only hit diagonal shots at goal.

Variations
1) The attacking players use a playmaker who must not shoot.
2) Place the goals on the diagonal line.
3) All players must play first time passes and head the ball to score.

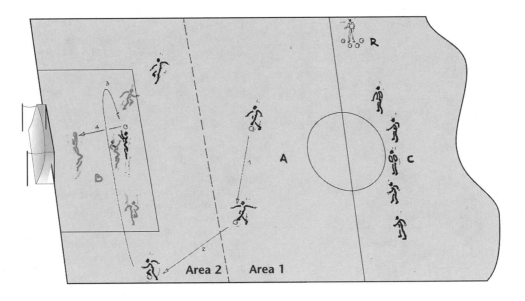

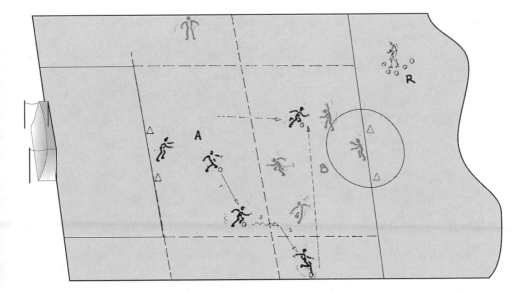

Exercise n. 128

Players
14.

Duration
15/20 minutes.

Objectives
1) Tactical play for the build-up to attacking moves preceding the shot.
2) Move the play from one area to another.

Description
Groups 7A and 7B play on the small pitch to attack the small 3-meter goals. They both play two-touch soccer and 1-2 combinations. In order to start the build-up of the attack the attacking team must pass one of the 15-meter areas at the center of the field.

Variations
1) The support players play in fixed positions at the bottom of the pitch between one goal and another.
2) The group in possession must move all its players into the opponents' area before shooting.
3) Finish inside 1 minute.
4) Alternate the attacking players with the defenders every 5 minutes.

Exercise n. 129

Players
10 + 1 goalkeeper.

Duration
15/20 minutes. The players change positions every 5 minutes.

Objectives
Tactical play based on three attacking players who function as playmakers for fast moves.

Description
Group 6A attacks the goal defended by the goalkeeper and group 4B on a small pitch. Group 6A plays three-touch soccer. Three of the players from group A build up the move with first time passes. They must finish with shots hit from outside the area. Each attacking move must be finished in under two minutes. If group B gains possession it must play to maintain possession for at least 1 minute with the help of the goalkeepers.

Variations
1) Three attacking players shoot from outside the area, two from the wings and one from inside the penalty area. The latter must dribble the ball free of his opponent.
2) One attacking player acts as playmaker while the others must shoot from close to the goal.
3) Shot at goal only when the attacking players are inside the penalty area.
4) If group A loses the ball group B moves into attack with the help of the goalkeeper.

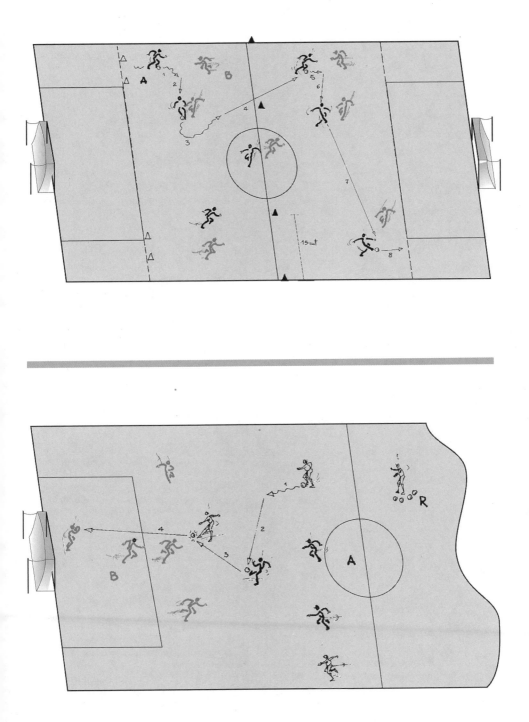

Exercise n. 130

Players
14 + 1 support players.

Description
The group builds up the attack moving across a 15-meter corridor with the ball to move in along the wing. The corridor is on the edges of the centerfield area, the support player moves from one area of the field to the other to send players in with long precise crosses.

Duration
20/25 minutes.

Variations
1) Passes to be played along the ground across the 30-meter opening.
2) The support players only play inside the areas marked with the dotted lines.
3) The support players act as playmakers in the attacking move.
4) Fast 1-2 moves and fast shots at goal.
5) 9 against 7, the 9 players are obligated to play first time passes.

Objectives
1) Build-up of the game moving the play from one area to another along the wings.
2) The playmaker's objective is to have clear vision over the entire field.

Exercise n. 131

Players
14 + 2 support players + 2 goalkeepers.

Description
Group 7A and 7B play each other for possession on a small pitch. They play 1-2 combinations and vary the passing. Each team moves from one half of the pitch to the other through a 30-meter opening in the center of the field. The areas marked by the dotted lines can only be crossed by the support players. Each group builds up its attack from the wings.

Duration
6/8 six minute sessions. 10/12 three minute sessions.

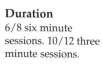

Variations
1) Passes to be played along the ground across the 30-meter opening.
2) The support players only play inside the areas marked with the dotted lines.
3) The support players act as playmakers in the attacking move.
4) Fast 1-2 moves and fast shots at goal.
5) 9 against 7, the 9 players are obligated to play first time passes.

Objectives
1) Continued attacking moves through numerous passes.
2) Movement of the ball and players.

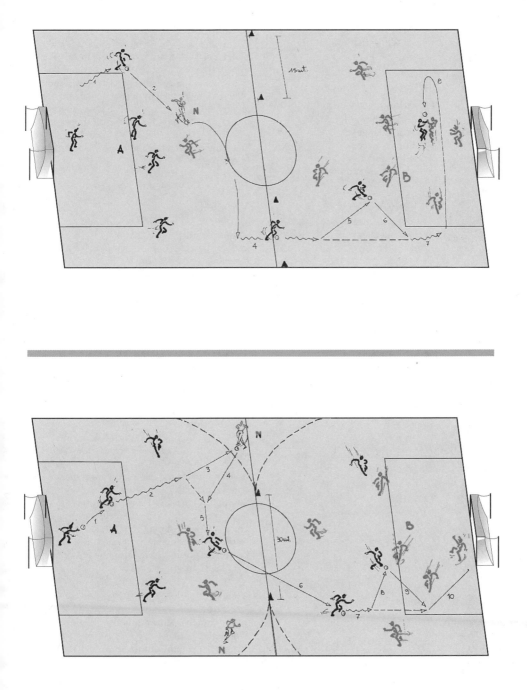

Exercise n. 132

Players
12 + 2 goalkeepers.

Duration
5/6 six minute sessions. Change of positions between defenders and attacking players every 6 minutes.

Objectives
Fast defensive technique to create an attacking move on the break.

Description
Group 3B attacks the 7-meter goals defended by the goalkeeper and group 3A. Group 3B is to play three-touch soccer and 1-2 combinations. When the defenders win possession they play it to their attacking players in area **2**, who are defended by group 3B. The shots at goal must be taken in under 30 seconds from outside the dotted line. In the 10-meter central area only one defender and one attacking player can play.

Variations
1) Game based on pressure play and long and short accurate passes.
2) A support player plays with the team that doesn't have possession.
3) Only the players inside the central area can shoot.
4) The player in possession inside the central area can move out but he must be substituted by another player.

Exercise n. 133

Players
16 + 2 goalkeepers.

Duration
6 five minute sessions.

Objectives
1) Tactical play based around the players in the central area. These players act as playmakers.
2) Adaptation to exchanges in offensive and defensive roles.

Description
Group 3A plays in area **1** to attack the goal defended by the goalkeeper and group 5B which plays three-touch soccer. One player from the attack and one player from the defense play inside the 10-meter area and play first time passes and 1-2 combinations with their teammates. At the same time in area **2** groups 3B and 5A play attack and defense respectively following the same rules. The move starts from a long throw by the keeper to the central area of the pitch.

Variations
1) Vary touches allowed with a preference for first time passes.
2) At R's signal the groups from each area get together to form two 8-man teams to attack the opponents' goals with the same rules of the two players inside the central area.

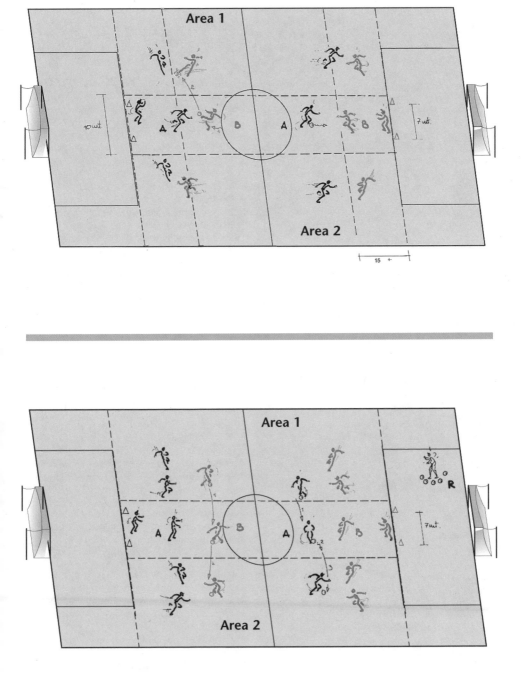

Exercise n. 134

Players
7 + 2 support players.

Duration
6 five minute sessions.

Description
Groups 4A and 3B play each other for possession on the small pitch marked **1**. They attack the small 4 meter goals. The two support players assist from the wings with first time passes. At R's signal group 4A moves the play around areas **1** and **2**. Group 3B defends both of the 3 meter goals playing three-touch soccer. They are assisted by the two support players who join the defense to make up 5 defenders against 4 attacking players.

Objectives
1) Tactical move to shift play from one small vertical area to another larger horizontal one.

Variations
1) Alternate the attacking group with the defending group.
2) At R's signal 5 attack and 3 defend.
3) The 5 players put the pressure on the attack
4) 5 against 3 in area **1** and 4 against 3 in areas **1** and **2**.

Exercise n. 135

Players
14 + 2 support players + 2 goalkeepers.

Duration
6 five minute sessions.

Description
Group 3A attacks the 6-meter goal defended by the goalkeeper and group 4B which plays only three-touch soccer. The same exercise is played in area **2** with group 3B attacking and group 4A defending. There is one support player in each area who both play on the right wing with the group in possession. At R's signal a defender from each group moves into the opponents' area of the field to assist with the attack.

Variations
1) Move play around the support player.
2) The defender who moves into the opponents' area of the field acts as a playmaker for the attack.
3) Only the support player shoots at goal.

Objectives
Tactical play to improve speed and adapt players to change of play.

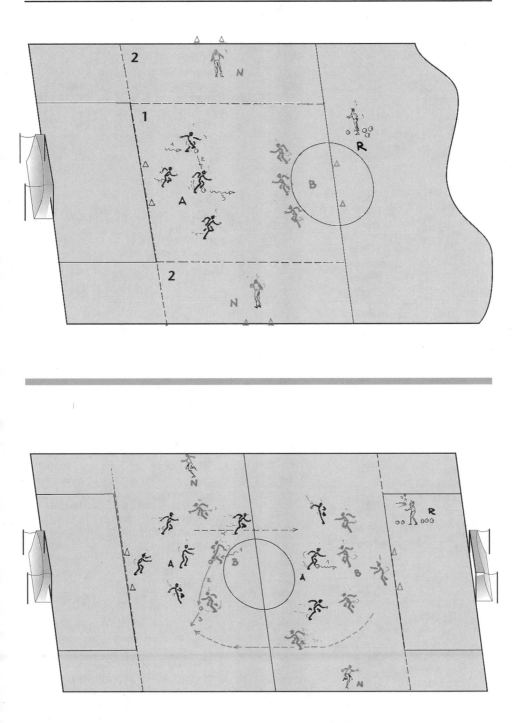

Exercise n. 136

Players
14 + 2 support players + 2 goalkeepers.

Duration
15/20 minutes.

Description
Groups 7A and 7B play to attack the goals defended by the goalkeepers. The players move down the wings to receive long accurate passes from the support player only. The teams should dribble and tackle in the central areas and move the ball around on the wings.

Variations
1) Attack on the break down the wings.
2) Only the support player can shoot.
3) 8 against 11 with the larger group attacking the two goals and the other playing to keep possession.

Objectives
1) Tactical play to create new openings and move the ball around with long accurate passes.
2) Fast moving game using all the space on the wings.

Exercise n. 137

Players
16 + 2 goalkeepers.

Duration
6 five minute sessions.

Description
Group 5B plays three-touch soccer to attack the 5-meter goal defended by the goalkeeper and group 3A in area **1**. The attacking group has a player who moves along the right wing of the pitch to assist the play with 1-2 combinations, long passes etc. The same exercise is done in area **2** with group 5A attacking and group 3B defending.

Variations
1) The attacking players play first time passes and a designated player is the only one who can shoot.
2) The player on the wing crosses the ball to the same player for a finishing header.
3) The goalkeeper joins the defense outside the goal.

Objectives
Tactical play to make defenders play fast passes and get in on the tackle.

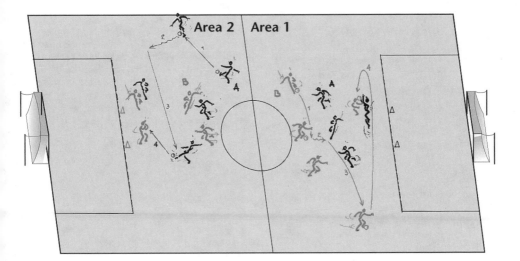

Exercise n. 138

Players
16 + 2 goalkeepers.

Duration
20/25 minutes.

Objectives
1) The defenders must get used to passing the ball to the midfield players in area **1**.
2) Play along the wings followed by an up and over cross for the final header.

Description
Groups 8A and 8B play each other on a regular pitch. The player in possession in area **1** sends a teammate on a run with a pass across a 5 meter area to move the play towards the wing. The move is to be finished with a header. A maximum of three attacking players and 2 defenders play in the central area **1**. The defending group plays two-touch soccer.

Variations
1) 10 against 8 with 2 support players who play along the wings.
2) All combinations in area **1** and two-touch soccer in the other areas.
3) Only dribbling of the ball in area **1** and open soccer in the other areas.
4) At R's signal a defender from one group becomes the attacker of the other group.

Exercise n. 139

Players
18 + 2 goalkeepers.

Duration
8/10 three minute sessions. All players change positions every three minutes.

Objectives
1) Tactical play to improve diagonal and vertical passing of the ball.
2) All players must cover open areas on the field.

Description
Groups 9A and 9B play each other for possession to attack the goals defended by the goalkeepers. Group A attacks and defends with diagonal and horizontal passes in areas **1** and **3** and plays two-touch soccer in area **2**. Group B plays vertical balls in area **2** and diagonal passes in areas **1** and **3**. The two groups must shoot every three minutes.

Variations
1) 2 support players start the move along the wings in area **2**.
2) Dribbling of the ball and shot from outside the area.
3) Invert the type of play in the three areas.

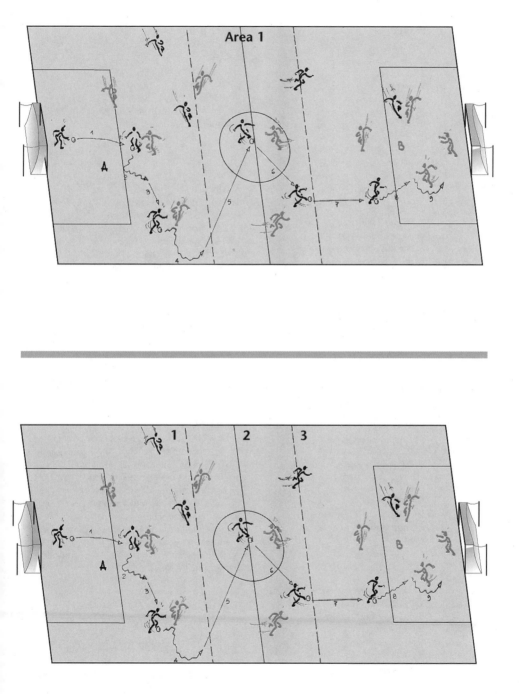

Exercise n. 140

Players
14 + 1 support player.

Duration
6/7 five minute sessions.

Objectives
1) High mobility of players of both groups to organize fast moves.
2) Fast changes of position to get away from opponent and keep possession.

Description
Group 6A attacks the four small 3-meter goals defended by group 8B on a small pitch. Group 8B plays three-touch soccer. The two support players assist group A in its build-up with first time passes while they assist group B with 1-2 combinations and attacking soccer to build up the move.

Variations
1) The support players play with the team that is not in possession.
2) The support players play with the defenders to make the attacking play more difficult.
3) Practice fast exchange of positions by alternating the defenders and the attacking players.

Exercise n. 141

Players
14 + 2 support players.

Duration
15 minutes. All players change position every 5 minutes.

Objectives
Build-up of fast attacking moves.

Description
Group 2B attacks the goal in area **1** defended by 5 players from group A, the two in goal playing only with their feet. In area **2** the roles are inverted with group B defending and group A attacking. The defenders from each group stay in their own area and play long balls to their attacking teammates with the help of the support players who play outside their area to assist the play with first time passes. The attacking players must hit shots along the ground within 2 minutes.

Variations
1) The two players in goal act as sweepers in the defense.
2) Limited touches for the bigger group.
3) At R's signal the support player with the ball can move into play and is substituted immediately by a defender.

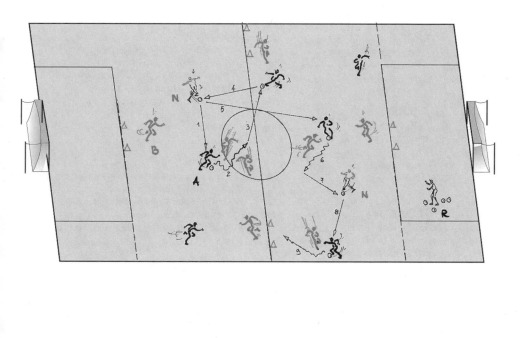

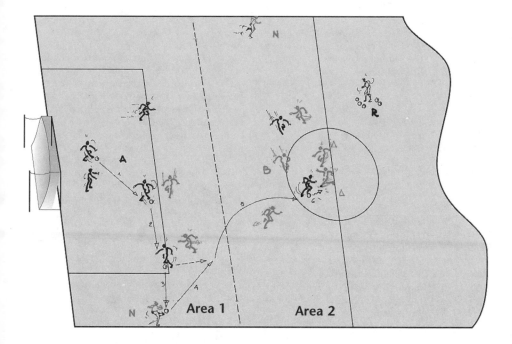

Exercise n. 142

Players
8 + 1 goalkeeper.

Duration
8/10 three minute sessions.

Objectives
1) The play centers around the playmaker in the midfield area who keeps the play moving with fast passes.
2) Diagonal shots to finish.

Description
Group 4A attacks the goal defended by the goalkeeper and group 4B on the small pitch. 1A plays as a playmaker in the central 10-meter area **1**. The shot must be hit under 1 minute only from area **2**.

Variations
1) Change of positions between groups A and B every three minutes.
2) Group B plays with a sweeper.
3) Vary the touches allowed.
4) Shot at goal from inside the central 10-meter area.

Exercise n. 143

Players
14 + 2 support players + 2 goalkeepers.

Duration
8/10 three minute sessions.

Objectives
1) Movement from one area to another to finish as quickly as possible.
2) The two teams move from the outside in through the two support players.

Description
Groups 7A and 7B play for possession on the small pitch. They both dribble the ball and tackle, three-touch soccer. They are assisted by two support players on the wings. The two support players play first time passes and 1-2 combinations. The team in possession must finish in under 2 minutes.

Variations
1) The support players play with the team that is not in possession.
2) The support players play with the defenders to make the attacking play more difficult.
3) Practice fast exchange of positions by alternating the defenders and the attacking players.

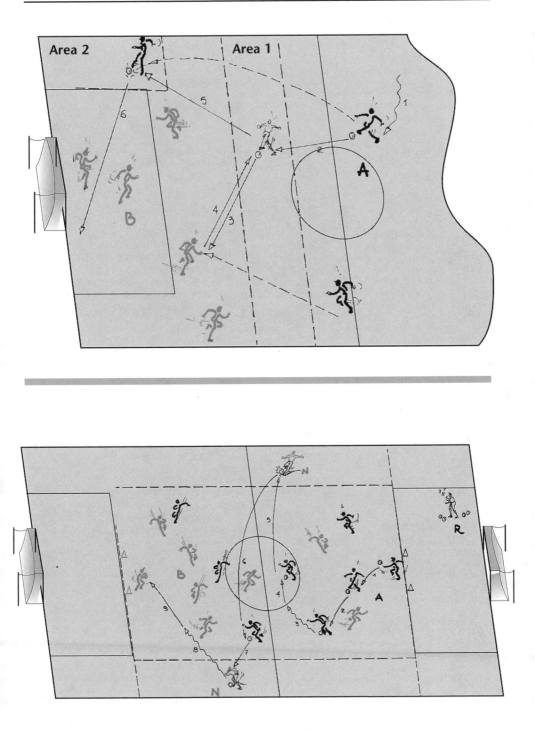

Exercise n. 144

Players
10 + 1 goalkeeper.

Duration
15/20 minutes.

Description
Group 4A plays three-touch soccer to attack the goal defended by group 2B and the goalkeeper on the small pitch. After going over the 20 meter area group A builds up the move along the wings to finish in under 1 minute. The finishing shot is hit by a designated player from the central area. If group A does not manage to finish in under 1 minute it is substituted by group C.

Objectives
Create new attacking moves for fast finishing.

Variations
1) 2B plays any combination and 4A plays two touch soccer.
2) During the attacking phase a defender and an attacking player rapidly change position.
3) The designated player can only score with a header.

Exercise n. 145

Players
12 + 1 goalkeepers.

Duration
6 five minute sessions.

Description
Group 4B attacks the 5-meter goal defended by the goalkeeper and group 2A on the small pitch **1**. Two of the players from the attacking group play on the wings. They are not tackled by the defenders and play long crosses and first time passes to their teammates. The same exercise is done in area **2** with group 4A attacking and group 2B defending. At a signal from R the players on the wings move to the center of the field to finish.

Objectives
1) Tactical move for incisive attacking play.
2) Particular attention is paid to the two players on the wings who act as playmakers.

Variations
1) The two players on the wings only shoot from a distance.
2) 1-2 combinations and finishing headers.
3) The defenders rapidly change positions with the attacking players during play.
4) At R's signal all the players from area **1** including the goalkeeper attack the goal in area **2** defended by the other 7.

20 m

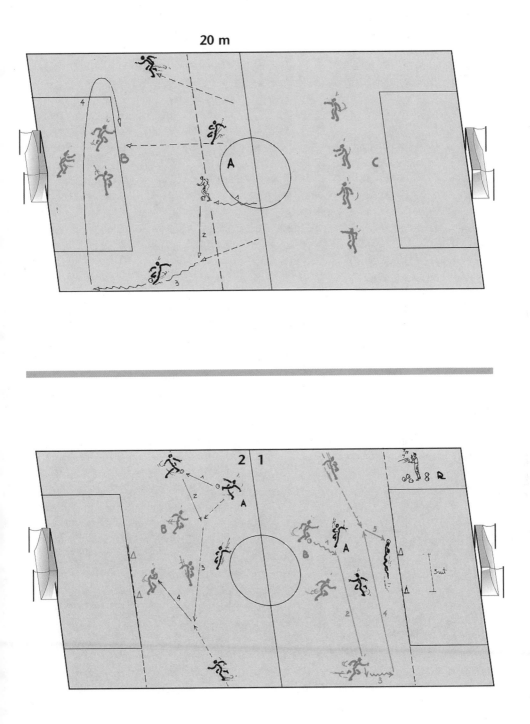

Exercise n. 146

Players
10 + 1 support player
+ 1 goalkeeper.

Duration
15/20 minutes. Change of positions between attacking players and defenders after every attacking move.

Objectives
Alternate defensive and offensive tactics for the development of specific characteristics.

Description
Group 3A and 2B and 3B and 2A play each other in areas **1** and **2**. At R's signal the player in possession in area **1** plays the ball to the support player in midfield. All the players from areas **1** and **2** move out to form teams in the following way: the players from group A move to defend the regular goal with a goalkeeper and the players from group B move to attack the goal and finish in under 1 minute. All players play two-touches.

Variations
1) A designated player is the only one allowed to shoot.
2) In area **1**, 3 play against 2 and in area **2**, 2 play against 1.
3) The attack builds up along the wings and the final shot is hit from outside the area.

Exercise n. 147

Players
14 + 2 goalkeepers.

Duration
10/12 attacking moves in each area.

Objectives
1) Tactical play for possession, dribbling and 1-2 combinations.
2) Long passes from one area to the other for fast adaptation of the players to defensive and offensive play.

Description
Group 4B plays two-touch soccer to attack the goal defended by group 2A and the goalkeeper on the small pitch **1**. At the same time in area **2** group 4A attacks the goal defended by group 2B and the goalkeeper. The defenders in each area have one of their defending teammates on the wing who cannot be tackled by the attacking players. This defender assists the play with first time passes. At R's signal he kicks the ball into the other area to his own teammates in attack to finish.

Variations
1) One player is designated to take the shot.
2) 2 support players are introduced to assist play with first time passes.
3) The three defenders alternate positions with the four attacking players.

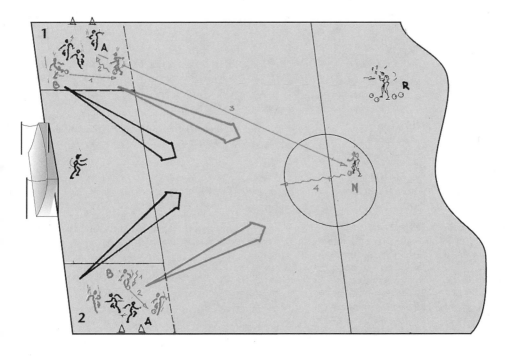

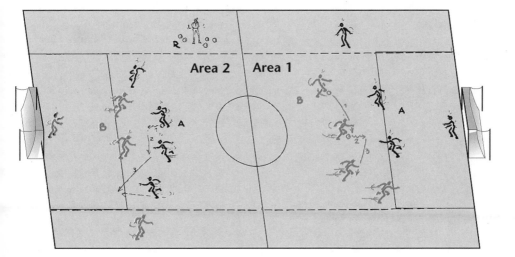

Exercise n. 148

Players
15 + 2 goalkeepers.

Duration
8/10 attacking moves for each group. After three attacking moves the group changes position with the defenders.

Objectives
1) Attack in both directions with moves from the wings and finishing shot from the center.
2) The play centers around a playmaker who assists the play and keeps the game moving.

Description
Group 5A plays first time passes to finish in under 40 seconds in area **1**. It attacks the goal defended by group 5B and the goalkeeper. Group 5B plays three-touch soccer. When the move is over group A repeats the move attacking the goal defended by group C and the goalkeeper in area **2**.

Variations
1) Finishing headers only.
2) Two playmakers and three strikers.
3) 2 support players stand on the edges of the pitch to play long high crosses.

Exercise n. 149

Players
12.

Duration
5 five minute sessions.

Objectives
Movement of the ball and players across the field.

Description
Group 3B dribbles the ball and plays diagonal passes to take the ball across the dotted line indicated in the diagram in area **1**. It is defended by group 2A. In area **2** group 3A attacks and group 2B defends. A single player from outside the pitch collaborates with the defending groups, 2A in area **1** and 2B in area **2**. He plays first time passes to both groups.

Variations
1) One group dribbles the ball to keep possession while the other has limited touches.
2) A support player in each area who acts as a playmaker.
3) The external player plays long crosses.

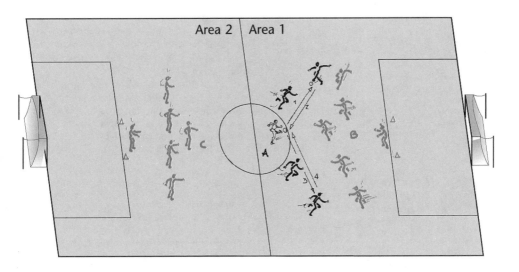

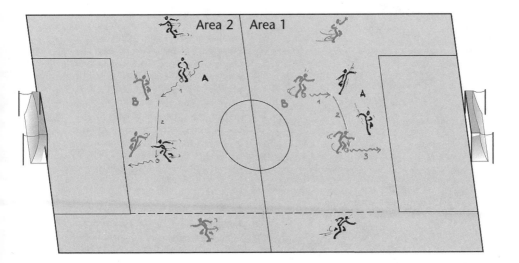

Exercise n. 150

Players
20.

Duration
20 minutes. The groups change areas every three minutes.

Objectives
1) Tactical move for improvement of short, fast, direct passes and for the movement of play from one area to another with surprise shots.
2) Adaptation of the groups to fast changes in play.

Description
The groups play to attack the small 3-meter goals in the areas **1, 2, 3, 4**. In area 1 group 3A attacks group 3B defends and is limited to two touches. In area **2** group 2A plays two-touch soccer to attack group 2B. In area **3** group 3A defends the two small goals from group 3B's attack. In area **4** play continues as in area **1**. At R's signal the groups from area **1** and **2** exchange balls and continue play inverting the rules. The same thing takes place in areas **3** and **4**.

Variations
1) Invert the rules of play for areas **1, 3** and **2, 4**.
2) A support player in each area with the role of passing the ball into the opposing area.
3) All the groups from all areas exchange passes with diagonal and vertical balls.

Exercise n. 151

Players
12.

Duration
10/12 eight minute sessions.

Objectives
Tactical play using the wing for fast exchanges.

Description
Group 2A attacks the goal defended by the goalkeeper and group 3B in area **1**. Group 3B plays three-touch soccer. A third attacking player plays along the wings to assist with two-touch soccer and long passes. At the same time in area **2** group 2B attacks and group 3A defends. Group 2B is assisted by a third player on the wing. The two players on the wings are not tackled by the defenders and must get rid of the ball within a few seconds.

Variations
1) The 6 players in area **1** attack the goal in area **2** defended by the goalkeeper and the other 6 players.
2) 6 defenders and 4 attacking players in each area.
3) Dribbling and pressure play.
4) Alternate attacking players and defenders every 2 minutes.

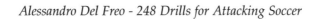

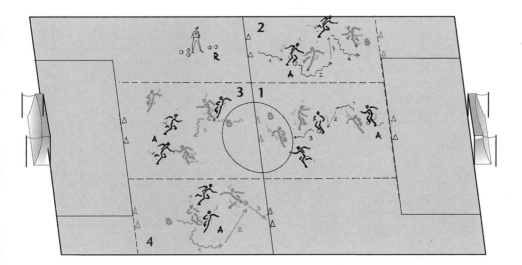

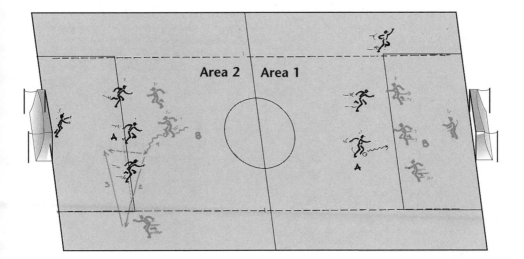

Exercise n. 152

Players
12.

Duration
Six 5 minute sessions.

Objectives
Development of
attacking moves.

Description
Groups 4A and 4B play to attack the small
goals on a small pitch. Group A plays three-
touch soccer. The two players from group A
outside the playing area assist with 1-2 combinations and can move in to play alternately for
a few seconds only.

Variations
1) Exchange of players outside the playing area
with the players on the pitch.
2) The two external players can shoot from
outside the playing area.
3) Two players from group B act as playmakers
without shooting at goal.

Exercise n. 153

Players
10 + 2 goalkeepers.

Duration
Six 5 minute sessions.

Objectives
Adaptation of the
players to horizontal
and vertical moves.

Description
Group 5B plays in the midfield area **1** to attack
the regular goal in midfield defended by group
A. When group A gains possession it attacks
the two small goals in area **2** defended by
group B.

Variations
1) Group A attacks the small goals with the
help of the goalkeepers.
2) A support player acts as defender.

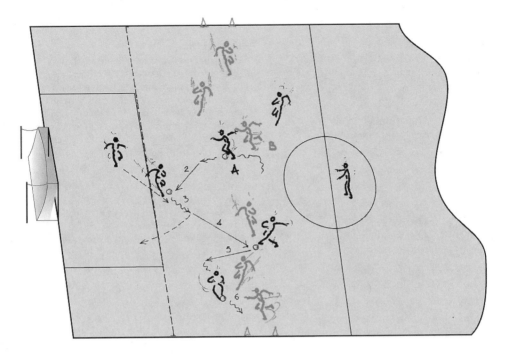

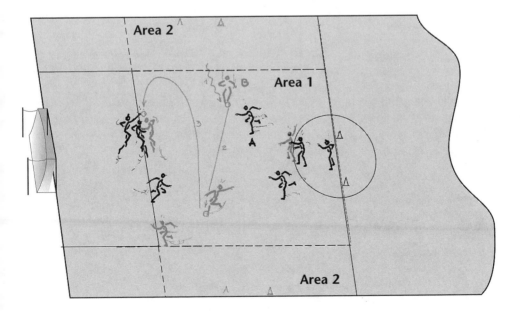

Exercise n. 154

Players
10 + 1 support player.

Duration
Six 3 minute sessions.

Objectives
Tactical play for immediacy in attack.

Description
Group 5A plays group 5B on a small pitch. The support player plays with the group in possession of the ball and acts as a playmaker. The team in possession attacks the three small 2-meter goals defended by the other group. The goals are set up on a triangular area measuring 10-meters on each side. Not all players can move into the triangle.

Variations
1) One team plays to shoot at goal while the other plays to keep possession.
2) Change of roles every three minutes.

Exercise n. 155

Players
16 + 1 support player + 1 goalkeeper.

Duration
Six 5 minute sessions.

Objectives
1) Each group attacks and defends in its own area.
2) Perfection of the attacking move through organization of the defense.

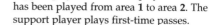

Description
Groups 5A and 5B play for possession in area **1**. The group in possession of the ball plays in into area **2** to its attacking teammates after a maximum of five passes. The 3 attacking players must finish in under 30 seconds. The support player moves into play after the ball has been played from area **1** to area **2**. The support player plays first-time passes.

Variations
1) Each group in its own area plays with a playmaker.
2) After each goal scored the direction of play is inverted from area **2** to area **1**.

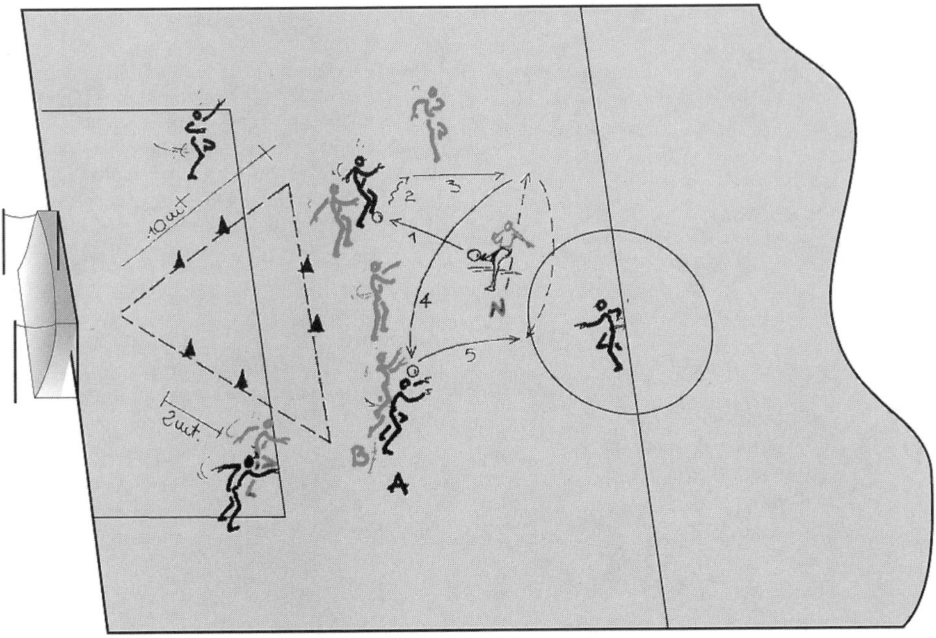
10 mt
2 mt
1
2
3
4
5
N
B
A

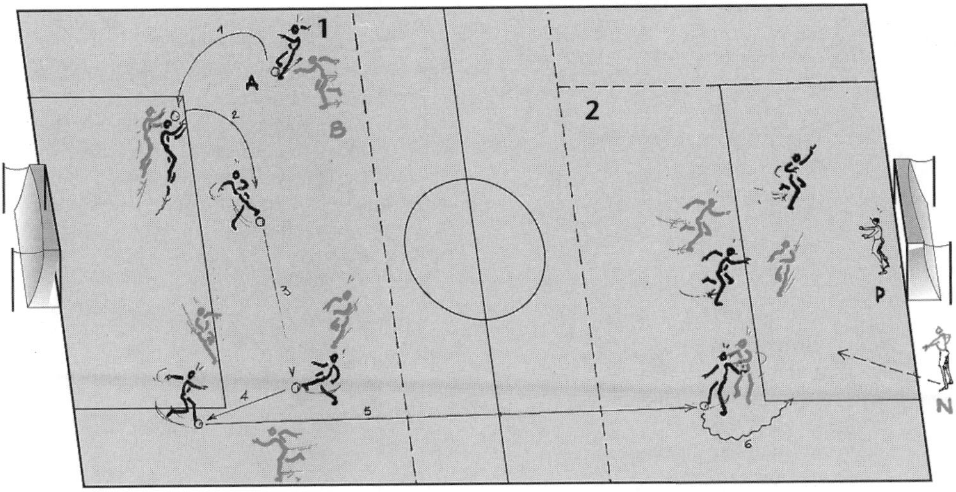
1
A
B
2
1
2
3
4
5
6
P
N

Exercise n. 156

Players
14 + 2 goalkeepers.

Duration
25 minutes.

Objectives
Co-ordinated move through fast runs of players.

Description
Groups 7A and 7B play each other for possession on a small pitch with 5-meter goals. When one team gains possession the move has to be started from a player who moves onto the wing. Each team can shoot when at least 4 of its players are in the opponent's half.

Variations
1) Introduction of two support players.
2) One team keeps possession and the other shoots.

Exercise n. 157

Players
16.

Duration
Eight 3 minute sessions.

Objectives
1) Rapid pass from one area to the other and speed of the move.
2) Capitalize on every advantage situation.

Description
In area **1** and **2** groups 4A and 4B play each other. The areas measure 25 x 35 meters. At R's signal the team in possession of the ball plays an accurate pass into the corresponding area: **1** to **1**, **2** to **2**. All players move quickly into the other area to gain possession of the ball and continue the exercise. The player who kicked the ball plays as a support player to assist the team in possession of the ball from outside the playing area.

Variations
1) A support player off the pitch.
2) A player from each group plays as a playmaker.

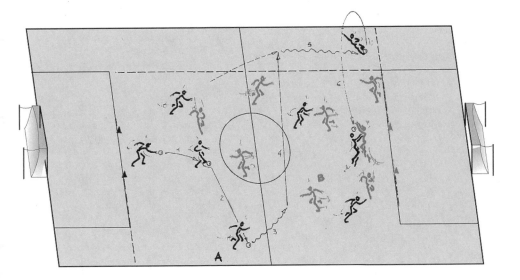

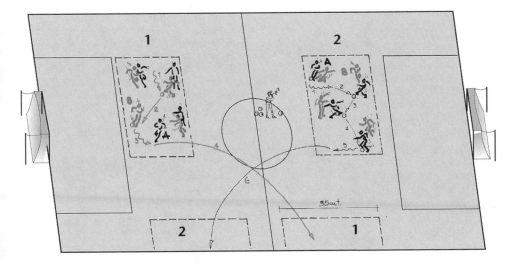

Exercise n. 158

Players
8.

Duration
Five 5 minute sessions.

Description
Groups 4A and 4B play on the three small pitches **1**, **2** and **3**. In area **1** the two groups play first time passes and have to finish in under 30 seconds in the small goals. In area **2** they dribble the ball and have to carry the ball across the goal line of the small goals in under 30 seconds. In area **3** the group that gains possession eliminates one of its players and has to score in under 20 seconds in the small goals.

Objectives
1) Improvement of dribbling and 1-2 combinations.
2) Fast passes for fast solutions.

Variations
1) Invert the direction of play.
2) Limit touches.
3) Pressure play in areas **1** and **2**.

Exercise n. 159

Players
10 + 2 support players + 2 goalkeeper.

Duration
20/25 minutes. Change of positions between players and support players every 5 minutes.

Description
Groups 5A and 5B play three-touch soccer on the small pitch. They both have to finish in under 1 minute. At R's signal 2 support players move into play to create fast attacking moves with first time passes and long passes. After scoring the teams continue play from R's throw. The goalkeepers move out from their goals and join in the attack.

Objectives
Players must free themselves continually from their opponents.

Variations
1) A support player plays with the group that doesn't have possession.
2) One of the groups plays three-touch soccer.
3) At R's signal a player from one of the groups moves to the other group to play 6 against 4.

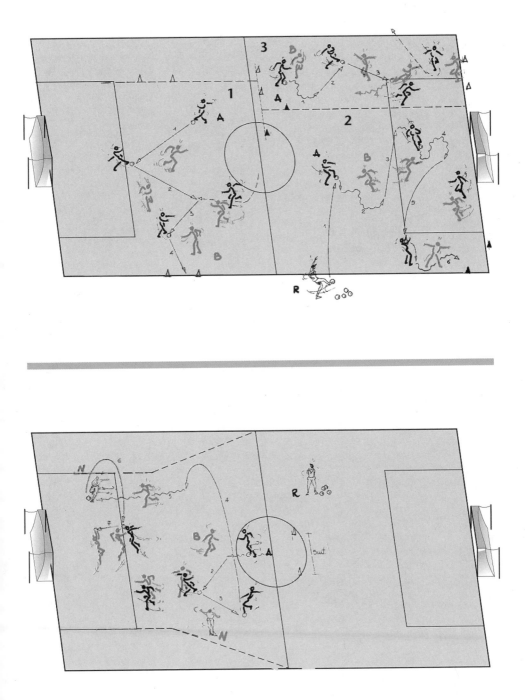

Exercise n. 160

Players
16 + 2 support players.

Duration
15/20 minutes.

Objectives
Evaluate the play with movement of players and ball.

Description
Group 3A and 3B play each other for possession in areas **1** and **2**. At R's signal the player in possession plays the ball to his teammate on the wing who, in turn, plays it into the opposite area for the play to continue. The two support players dribble the ball and use the players on the wing to play first time passes and speed up the game.

Variations
1) One group plays three-touch soccer to keep possession and the other dribbles the ball.
2) Only the support player can receive the ball from the player on the wing to play it into the opposite area.

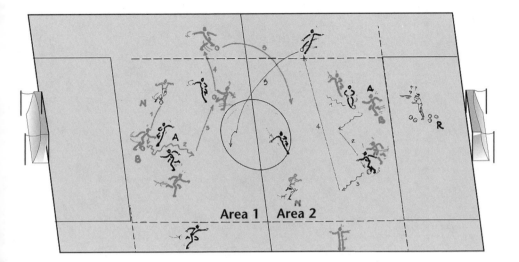

Area 1   Area 2

CHAPTER FOUR

Tactical moves in confined spaces to create fast solutions for finishing shots on goal

1) Collective moves to develop flow of the move through execution of technique
2) Finishing moves on a series of goals
3) Tactical moves in different areas and in opposite areas.

This phase of the training program introduces complex procedures for technique. The exercises involved are designed to enhance the motor abilities of the individual. This is a fundamental component for improved team play. Their aim is to increase the ability of the player regarding muscle and nerve capacity so as to reach maximum technical impulse for the correct execution of shots. This move requires perfect control of the ball, succes-

sive movements, speed and strength. The player's goal is perfecting the various components of the technical and tactical procedures and the rhythm of their execution. The coach will regulate the level of play and make sure the exercises are carried out with the correct regularity and input so that they become an integral part of the motor functions of the athlete.

Exercise n. 161

Players
14 + 1 support player
+ 1 goalkeeper.

Duration
30/40 passes to the
support player. Every 5
shots A-B-C-D and N
change positions.

Objectives
Perfection of precision
of shots through flow of
the move.

Description
The support player crosses the ball in from the
corner for A who heads the ball out of the area
to C. C plays a first time ball to D who hits a
volley. B attempts to interfere with A, C, and
D's play.

Variations
1) A plays to D who touches on to C for the
final shot.
2) N plays to D for A who plays a first time
ball to C for the shot.
3) The support player plays a short ball to A.
He frees himself from B and plays into space
for C and D who finish.

Exercise n. 162

Players
16.

Duration
Six 5 minute sessions.
Every 5 minutes the
defenders and the
attacking players
change positions.

Objectives
1) Development of tacti-
cal maneuvers to con-
solidate and support the
offensive and defensive
play.
2) Practice quick change
in defensive and attack-
ing play.

Description
Group 4A plays two-touch soccer to attack the
5-meter goals defended by the goalkeeper and
group 4B in area **1**. In area **2** group 4B attacks
the goal defended by the goalkeeper and
group 4A. Every minute the group in possession has to shoot. At R's signal the groups
exchange balls between one area and the other
and whoever gains possession attacks the goal
in its own area defended by the other group.

Variations
1) A playmaker in each area who doesn't shoot.
2) Build-up of the move from the wings and
first time shot.
3) A support player in the corner who assists
the play with long passes.

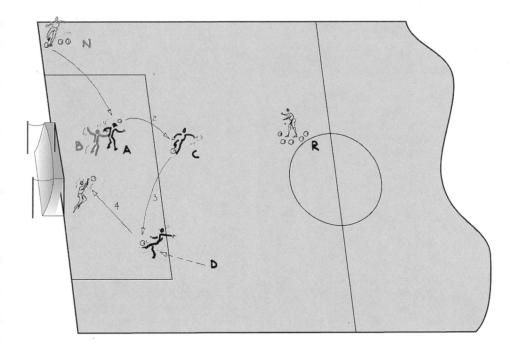

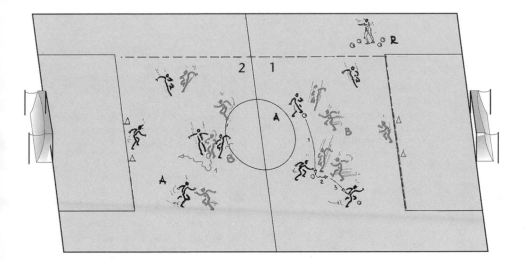

Exercise n. 163

Players
10.

Duration
15 minutes. The players change pairs every five minutes.

Objectives
1) Fast movement of the players to free themselves from the opponent.
2) Fast movement of the ball for rapid attacking moves.

Description
Groups 5A and 5B play for possession on the small pitch. They both dribble the ball to shoot at the small goals. The player in possession is attacked by only one of the other players (exercise in pairs). The ball is moved around between the players in each group with short runs and diagonal passes.

Variations
1) At R's signal a support player comes into play to join the team that is not in possession.
2) A support player comes into play with the group in possession to play as a playmaker.
3) One group plays to keep possession, the other to attack the two goals.
4) One player from each group stays in one of the corners to play first times passes.
5) When a player loses the ball he stops and play continues 5 against 4.

Exercise n. 164

Players
18 + 1 goalkeeper.

Duration
15/20 minutes. Every minute R alternates the groups for the delivery of the ball to area **3**.

Objectives
Co-ordination of individual moves and team play for organized tactical play.

Description
Group 4A and 4B play each other in areas **1** and **2**. They send the ball across a 20-meter area on the edges of the pitch. At R's signal the player with the ball in area **1** plays it to his teammate in area **3** who moves to shoot at the regular goal defended by the goalkeeper. His opponent tries to dispossess him. R alternates the groups in the two areas when throwing the ball into play and throws another ball into the area left without a ball.

Variations
1) A support player in area **3** to speed up play.
2) At R's signal the player with the ball moves into area **3** and attacks the goal with his teammate. The goal is defended by the player from the other group and the goalkeeper.
3) The groups play three-touch soccer in areas **1** and **2** and dribble the ball in area **3**.

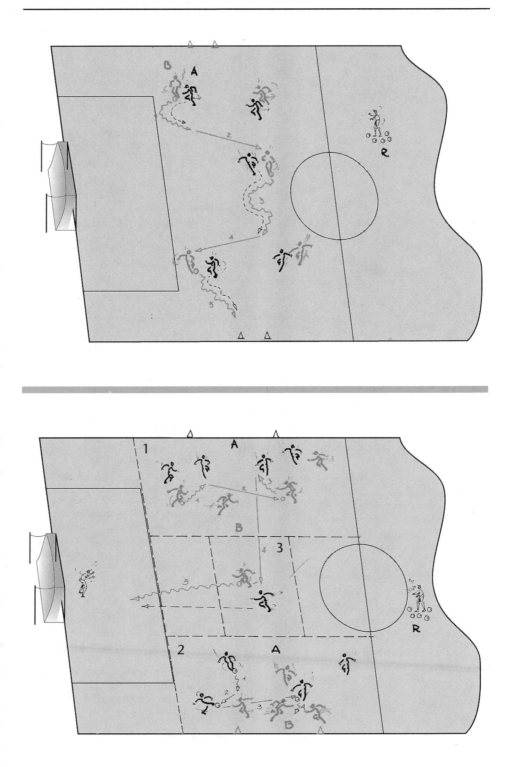

Exercise n. 165

Players
2 + 1 support player
+ 1 goalkeeper.

Duration
20/25 shots.

Description
From the support player's corner A and B move from different positions to head at goal. A moves from the edge of the box and B from the goal line. The exercise is repeated from the other corner with another support player and C and D. After each move the players change position.

Variations
1) The players A-B and C-D shoot to finish.
2) The players B and D move into play in advance for the finish.
3) The support players pass the ball from the edge of the box.

Objectives
Motor dynamism for the development of speed of movement and technique.

Exercise n. 166

Players
4.

Duration
15/20 minutes.

Description
The players A and B stand 8 meters apart, they move forward playing rapid, diagonal passes to each other. At R's signal the player in possession dribbles the ball to attack the 2-meter goal on the side of the pitch. The goal is defended by the other player. The exercise is repeated by the pair C-D at the same time.

Objectives
Fast build-up of an attacking move through fast, first time passing of the ball.

Variations
1) At R's signal a support player moves into play to play 1-2 combinations.
2) Four players 2A and 2B start the exercise. At R's signal two attack and two defend, all players dribble the ball.
3) The goal is defended by a goalkeeper who only uses his feet.
4) Alternate the attacking player with the defender.

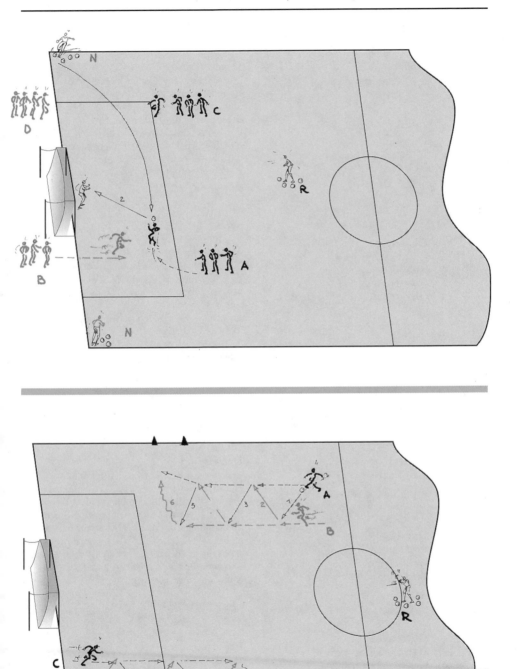

Exercise n. 167

Players
6 + 2 support players.

Duration
25/30 corners from both sides.

Description
The support player hits a long, high cross in from the corner. Group 3A takes the ball down and creates an attacking move on the goal defended by the goalkeeper. Group 3B comes in from off the pitch when the support player hits the corner to defend the goal. If group B wins possession the roles are inverted. Group B with the support player as playmaker attacks and group A defends.

Objectives
Coordination of technique and tactical ability for creation of fast attacking moves.

Variations
1) When the defenders gain possession they pass it to the support player who starts an attacking move which is to be finished in under 30 seconds.
2) Only the designated player from group A is allowed to shoot.
3) The defenders mark and the attacking players dribble the ball.

Exercise n. 168

Players
6 + 1 goalkeeper.

Duration
15/20 minutes. Every three minutes all players change positions.

Description
Group 2A and 2B play each other on a small pitch 1, to keep possession. They both dribble the ball and play 1-2 combinations. R throws the ball into area 1 and the player who wins possession passes it to his teammate in area 2 or area 3. This player moves forward rapidly to shoot diagonally from outside the dotted line. The two players inside areas 2 and 3 do not come into play in area 1.

Objectives
1) Fast attacking move on the goal with diagonal shot.
2) Tactical phase to improve technique of execution.

Variations
1) A support player in area 1 for first time passes.
2) In area 1 group A dribbles the ball and group B marks.
3) During the game the player from area 2 or 3 can move into area 1 to participate in the move. He is immediately substituted by a teammate.

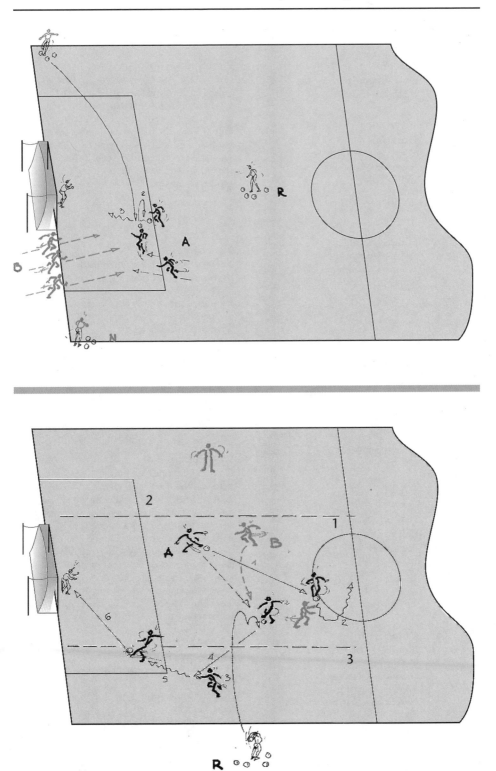

Exercise n. 169

Players
6 + 2 support players + 1 goalkeeper.

Duration
25/30 corners shots in succession from the support players.

Objectives
Series of individual actions and team-play for basic tactics.

Description
From the support player's corner A heads the ball over the dotted line to group 3B. This group attacks the goal defended by group 3A and the goalkeeper. Group B plays fast passes and dribbles the ball when it goes past the dotted line. The attack is directed by a playmaker who assists the finish in under 1 minute from the other two players. Every three minutes the groups change positions.

Variations
1) The support player who hits the corner moves into play to mark with the defense.
2) The attacking group builds up the attack from the center of the penalty area.
3) The 2 support players join with each group after the corner kick.

Exercise n. 170

Players
20.

Duration
15 minutes.

Objectives
1) Build-up for tactical moves.
2) Technical tactical development of players in difficult situations of play.

Description
On the small pitch **1** a player B attacks the goal defended by the goalkeeper and two defenders A. At the same time outside the penalty area group 4B plays three-touch soccer to keep possession, while group 3A attempts to dispossess it. At R's signal group 4B attacks the goal defended by group 3A. Group 4B can only shoot from outside the area. At the same time in area **2** the same exercise is carried out with 1A attacking and 2B defending in the penalty area. The other two groups 4A and 3B stay in the other area.

Variations
1) The single player inside the area dribbles the ball to finish.
2) At R's signal groups 5A and 5B unite to finish rapidly.
3) At R's signal all players use all combinations.

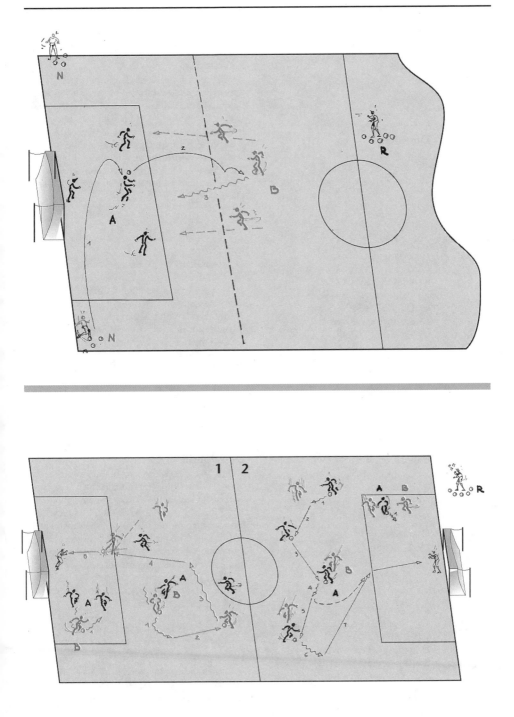

Exercise n. 171

Players
7 + 1 goalkeepers.

Duration
15 minutes.

Description
Group 3B dribbles the ball and plays diagonal passes to defend the two 3-meter goals in midfield and attack the goal defended by the goalkeeper and group 4A. At R's signal a player from group A moves rapidly to play with group B to finish in the regular goal with a shot from outside the area in under 30 seconds. Each time a group gains possession it must start the attack from the player designated as playmaker.

Objectives
Quick adaptation of players to tactical changes in play for the development of specific characteristics for attacking and defensive moves.

Variations
1) Group B attacks all the goals and group A plays to defend.
2) Groups A includes the goalkeeper to maintain possession.
3) 5 against 5 with support players standing on the edges of the pitch to play first time passes to keep the ball moving.

Exercise n. 172

Players
5 + 2 support players + 1 goalkeeper.

Duration
15/20 minutes.

Description
Group 3B defends the two small 3 meter goals on the halfway line and attacks the 5 meter goal defended by the goalkeeper and group 2A. If group 2A gains possession, it attacks the two small goals against 2B and the move has to be finished with a shot in under 30 seconds. The 2 support players play first time passes and assist fast finishing moves.

Objectives
1) Tactical continuity for fluidity in play.
2) Alternation between defense and attack for the development of specific characteristics.

Variations
1) At R's signal the 2 support players come onto the field to play with team A and the exercise continues 4 against 3.
2) 2A plays without restrictions and 3B plays three-touch soccer.
3) A keeper defends the two goals in midfield.

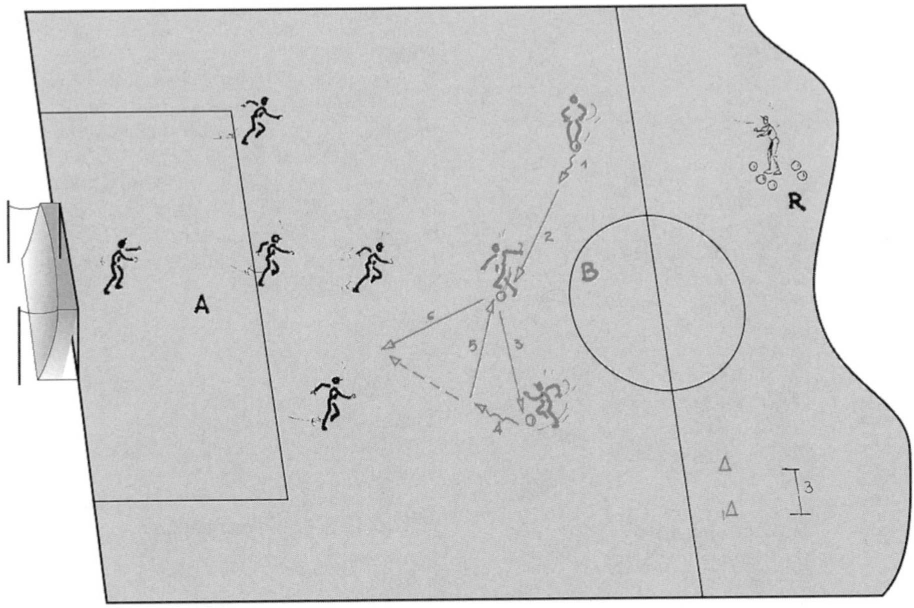
A
B
R
1
2
3
4
5
6
3

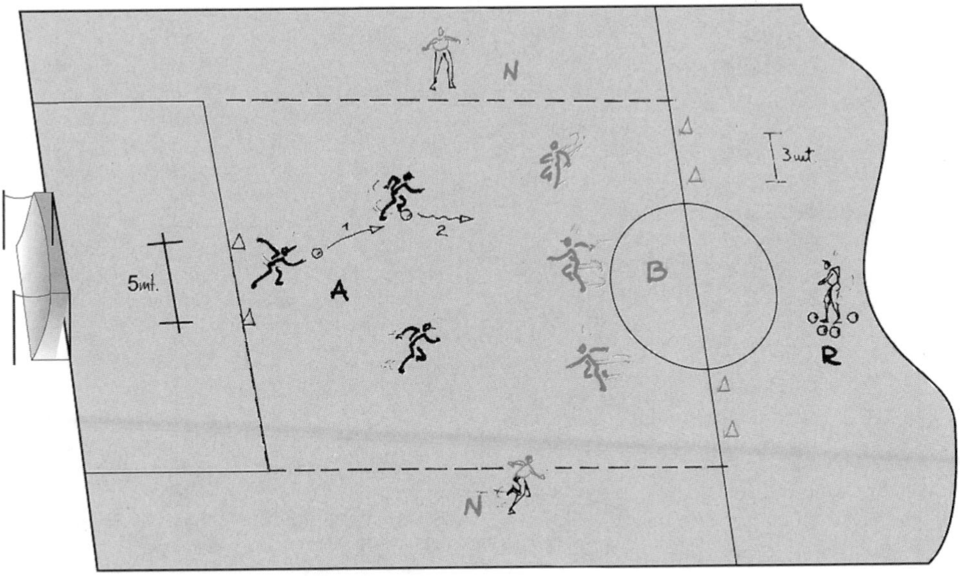
N
3mt.
1
2
5mt.
A
B
R
N

Exercise n. 173

Players
24.

Duration
18 minutes. Players move from one area to another every 3 minutes.

Objectives
1) Groups are widely distributed to allow greater movement on the pitch.
2) Tactical game to improve changes of position and dribbling techniques.
3) Fast control and possession for fast finishing.

Description
Groups 3A and 3B play in areas **1**, **2**, **3** and **4**. One group attacks the small 3 meter goals and the other group defends. At R's signal the groups from each area exchange balls with long passes played as follows: **1** to **4** and **2** to **3** to continue play with first time touches, dribbling of the ball and tight marking. No player must enter the central area of the pitch indicated by the dotted lines.

Variations
1) Two support players play in midfield to assist play with first time passes.
2) Limited touches and at R's signal all players go back to using all combinations.

Exercise n. 174

Players
7 + 1 goalkeeper.

Duration
15/20 attacking moves. Attacking players and defenders change positions every 2 minutes.

Objectives
Tactical freedom for players who have to finish in under 30 seconds.

Description
On the small pitch group 3A attacks the goal defended by the goalkeeper and group 4B. Group 3A plays 1-2 combinations and dribbles the ball. In group A one of the defenders acts as a playmaker and in group B one of the defenders acts as a sweeper at the center of the box. Group A has to finish in under 30 seconds. If group B gains possession it has to maintain possession for 1 minute inside the penalty area with first time passes, 1-2 combinations, dribbling of the ball etc.

Variations
1) During the attacking move one of the defenders at R's signal becomes an attacking player, this player must finish in under 1 minute.
2) 4 attacking players of which 2 are playmakers, are marked by three defenders. The playmakers cannot shoot.
3) 2 support players outside the wings for long and short first time passes.

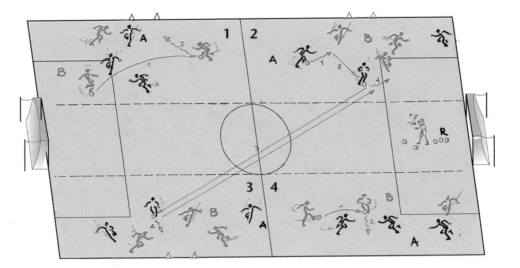

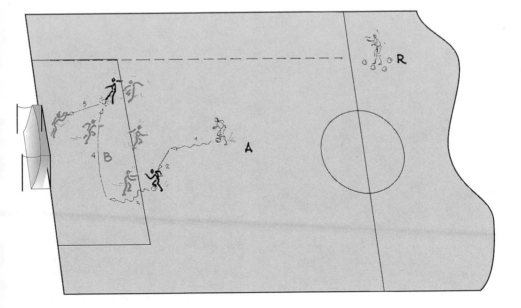

Exercise n. 175

Players
7 + 2 goalkeepers.

Duration
15/20 attacking moves. Change of position between groups every 5 minutes.

Objectives
1) Tactical play for the attacking group that has no inferior number of players.
2) Change of play from one area to another for rapid change of tactics from attacking to defensive play.

Description
Groups 3A attacks the 5-meter goal defended by the goalkeeper and group 4B in area **2**. Group 3A dribbles the ball and uses various combinations while group 4B plays three-touch soccer. When group B wins possession it moves to area **1** to attack the goal defended by group A and the goalkeeper. During the attacking move a player from group B moves to play as a defender with group A.

Variations
1) All players must pass the halfway line before finishing.
2) A support player comes on and off the field alternating with the attacking players.
3) When the defending players gain possession they move into the opposite area to receive a long pass from their own area of the field.

Exercise n. 176

Players
8 + 1 support player.

Duration
Six 5 minute sessions. Change between groups and the support player every 5 minutes.

Objectives
1) Alternation of attacking and defensive moves to improve specific characteristics.
2) Rapid passing with change of position.

Description
In area **1** group 2A plays attacking soccer and group 2B defends and in area **2** 2B against 2A. The support player plays in the 10-meter area in the center of the field. The game starts from the defender who plays the ball to the support player in the neutral area. The support player plays a long ball to the attacking players of the same group in the opposite area. The attacking players must dribble the ball across one of the 5-meter goals on the sides of the pitch.

Variations
1) Attack first in one direction then in the other. After three moves attacking players change positions with defenders.
2) 4 attacking players play two-touch soccer against 3 defenders who play all combinations in areas **1** and **2**.
3) 2 support players in the central area. One can move out of the area to play with groups A and B in both areas.

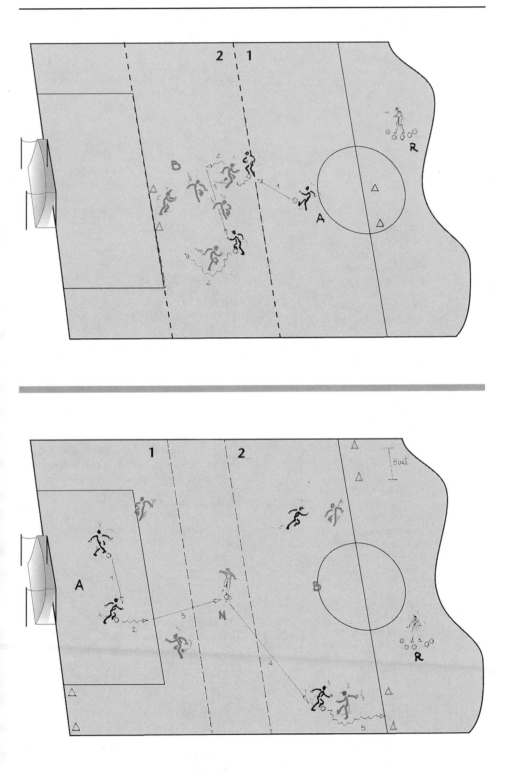

Exercise n. 177

Players
16 + 2 support players + 2 goalkeepers.

Duration
15/20 minutes.

Objectives
Adaptation of the players to rapid changes of attacking and defensive moves (rapid change of positions, freeing themselves of their opponents, keeping possession etc.).

Description
Groups 8A and 8B play against each other on a regular pitch to shoot. No player in possession can enter the 30-meter area in the center of the pitch. Each group builds up its own attack moving from one half to the other and playing long diagonal balls (group A from areas **3** and **4** to areas **1** and **2** and group B from areas **1** and **2** to ares **3** and **4**). The two support players play as playmakers both in attacking and defensive moves. The support players deliver fast passes and play 1-2 combinations.

Variations
1) The defenders from each group participate in the attacking moves in the opponents' half of the field without shooting.
2) Shots from outside the box.
3) The defenders play with two sweepers and the attacking players only shoot from outside the area.

Exercise n. 178

Players
8 + 1 goalkeeper.

Duration
Five 5 minute sessions. The players change positions every 5 minutes.

Objectives
Tactical move to improve the attack through first time passes, 1-2 combinations and dribbling.

Description
Group 4A plays two-touches, 1-2 combinations and dribbles the ball to attack the goal defended by group 2B and the goalkeeper. At R's signal two players move onto the pitch (one from off the goal-line, the other from the halfway line) to mark with the defenders. Group A must finish in under 30 seconds after all the players have touched the ball.

Variations
1) The shot is taken after all the attacking players have touched the ball, from the center of the field by a designated player.
2) The attacking players use three touches.
3) A fifth attacking player comes into play with the two defenders. The attacking player shoots from outside the area.

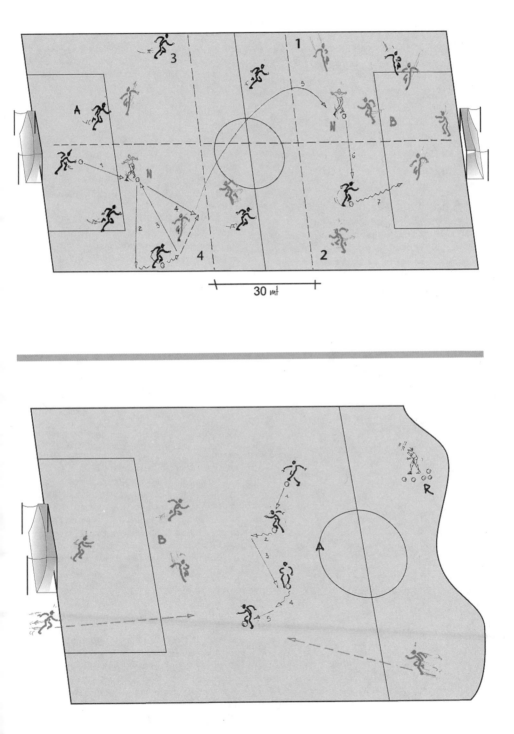

30 mt

Exercise n. 179

Players
17 + 2 goalkeepers.

Duration
15/20 minutes.

Objectives
The players must move across the central area which is neutral, stop there and carry the game forward from one side of the field to the other.

Description
Group 9A plays group 8B on a regular pitch. Each group has a 15-meter area in its own half. No player in possession can enter this area.

Variations
1) The bigger team must finish in under 2 minutes without the help of the defenders.
2) The opposing team must make three passes in its own area before attacking if it gains possession.
3) The playmakers can move into the 15 meter areas indicated by the dotted lines to free themselves of their opponents.
4) Change the bigger group with the other group every 5 minutes.

Exercise n. 180

Players
16 + 2 support players + 2 goalkeepers.

Duration
15/20 minutes.

Objectives
The players must move across the central area which is neutral, stop there and carry the game forward from one side of the field to the other.

Description
Groups 8A and 8B play each other for possession on a regular pitch. No player may enter the central rectangular area if he is in possession of the ball. Each group builds up its attack by playing long, diagonal passes from one half to the other (group A from areas **3** and **4** to areas **1** and **2** and group B from areas **1** and **2** to areas **3** and **4**). The two support players play as playmakers both in attack and in defense. They play quick passes and 1-2 combinations.

Variations
1) All players of the group with the ball must pass the halfway line before shooting.
2) 5 against 5 + 4 support players
3) One group plays to keep possession and defend, the other to attack both goals.
4) Only one player can move into the neutral area with the ball but he must move out quickly.

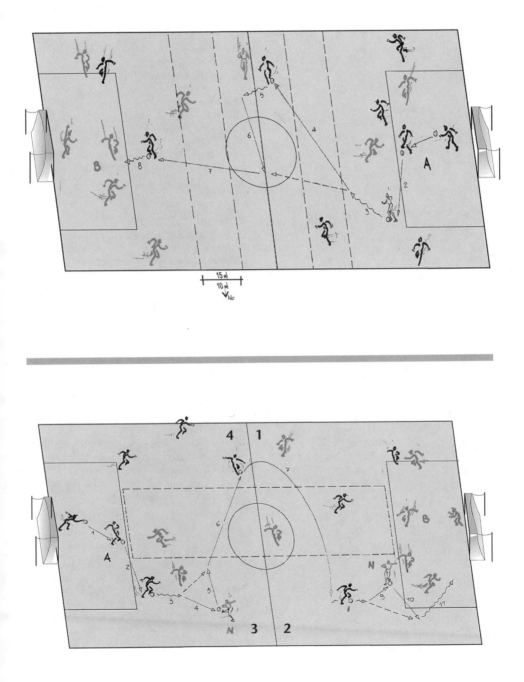

Exercise n. 181

Players
8 + 1 support player.

Duration
Six 5 minute sessions. Every minute the players change positions.

Description
Group 2A defends and group 2B attacks in area **1** and in **2** 2B against 2A. A support player plays in the 10-meter central area. The game builds up from the defender of one group who passes the ball to the support player in the neutral area. The support player delivers a long ball to the attacking players of the same group in the opposite area to attack the goal defended by the other group. The support player must pass the ball on rapidly.

Objectives
1) Tactical move to speed up the finish in the attack.
2) First time passing and dribbling.

Variations
1) Long high ball from the support player for finishing header.
2) 3 attacking players against 3 defenders in each area.
3) When the attacking players receive the pass from the support player they must finish in under 30 seconds.

Exercise n. 182

Players
12 + 2 goalkeepers.

Duration
15/20 minutes.

Description
Group 7A defends the goal with the two goalkeepers from group 5B which plays two-touch soccer. Group B must move into one of the indicated areas to dribble the ball and play 1-2 combinations before shooting.

Variations
1) Two-touch soccer inside the indicated areas.
2) A support player as a playmaker.
3) Enter the indicated area and dribble the ball out.
4) Limit touches.
5) Alternate the groups every 5 minutes, 7 attacking players and 5 defenders.

Objectives
1) Group 7A must use the entire field and dribble the ball.
2) Movement of players and ball for intensive play.

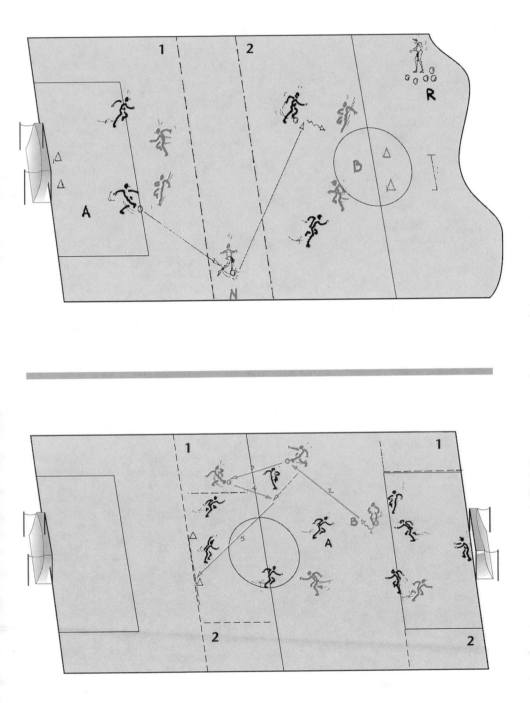

Exercise n. 183

Players
8 + 1 support player.

Duration
Six 5 minute sessions
Change between
groups and the support
player every 5 minutes.

Objectives
Fast finishing dribbling
the ball.

Description
2A defend and 2B attack in area **1**. 2A attack
and 2B defend in area **2**. A support player
plays in the 10-meter area in the center. The
exercise starts from a defender of one group
who passes the ball to the support player in
the neutral area. The support player delivers a
long ball to the attacking players of the same
group in the opposite area who must dribble
the ball across the line of the 7-meter goal
defended by the other group.

Variations
1) 3 defenders and 3 attacking players in each
area plus 2 support players in the central area.
2) A support player in areas **1** and **2**.
3) Two players in goal who defend with their
feet.
4) At R's signal the groups from each area
change positions (the defenders become
attackers and vice versa).

Exercise n. 184

Players
10.

Duration
4/5 five minute
sessions.

Objectives
1) Fast change of play
from the defender to the
attacking player and
rapid finishing.
2) Movement of the
players and the ball and
dribbling, 1-2 combina-
tions and first time
passes etc.

Description
Group 2B dribbles the ball to attack the small 3
meter goal in area **1** which is defended by
group 3A which plays three-touch soccer. In
area **2** group 3B defends and group 2A attacks.
The ball is passed from one area to the other
from the defenders to their attacking teammates. Only long passes are to be played.

Variations
1) The defenders mark tightly.
2) The attacking players must play 1-2
combinations before shooting.
3) At R's signal 3 attack and 2 defend.

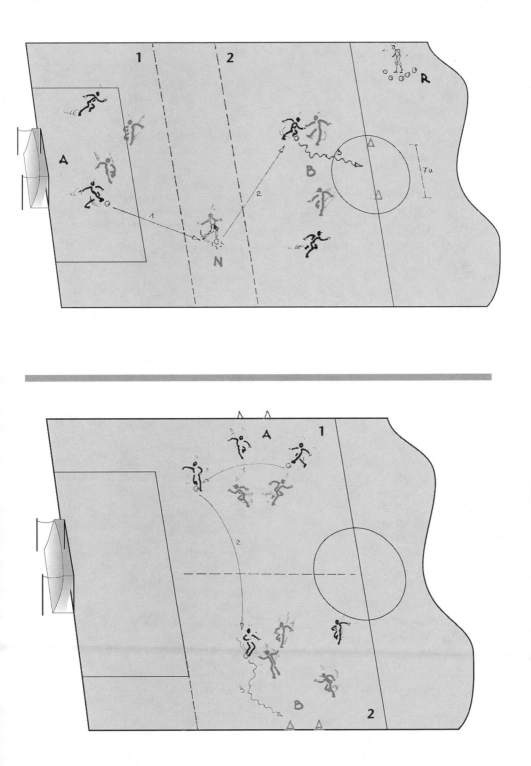

Exercise n. 185

Players
8.

Duration
4/5 five minute
sessions.

Objectives
Fast change in tactical
play for rapid defensive
and attacking moves.

Description
Group 4A plays group 4B for possession on a
small pitch. At R's signal the group in possession of the ball must attack the opponents' goal
in under 1 minute. The attacking group plays
two-touch soccer. The goal is defended by the
other group who mark tightly.

Variations
1) 3 against 4 dribbling the ball.
2) Shot after a 1-2 combination.
3) 5 against 3 and a support player as a
playmaker.
4) Shot after dribbling.

Exercise n. 186

Players
16 + 2 goalkeepers.

Duration
8/10 two minute
sessions.

Objectives
Tactical exercise based
on the playmakers who
speed up the move with
first time passes and
shots along the ground.

Description
Group 4A, with 2 playmakers, attacks the 5
meter goal defended by the goalkeeper and
group 4B in area **1**. In area **2** the roles are
inverted with 4A defending and 4B attacking.
The defenders of each group pass to their
teammates in the opposing areas through the
playmakers. The attacking players play three-
touches and have to finish in under 2 minutes.
Only the playmakers can shoot and they must
shoot from outside the area.

Variations
1) Alternate the players who act as playmakers
every 2 minutes in the attacking move.
2) Limit the defenders' touches.
3) 5 defenders against 6 attacking players and
2 support players.

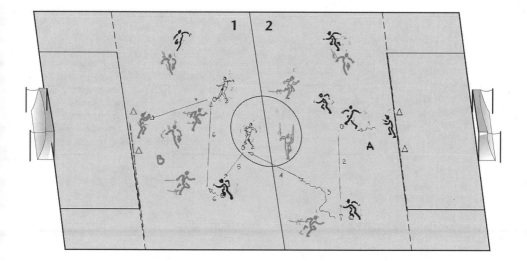

Exercise n. 187

Players
16 + 2 support players + 2 goalkeepers.

Duration
15/20 minutes.

Objectives
Movement of the play from one area of the field to the other through the two support players.

Description
Groups 8A and 8B play each other for possession on the small pitch. Two support players assist the play without being tackled. They both play on the wing and deliver first time passes. At R's signal a support player moves out to join in the play and is immediately substituted by another player of the same group.

Variations
1) 3 attacking players and 3 defenders play in the penalty area.
2) Limit the touches of the ball.
3) The support player acts as playmaker and can only shoot from outside the area.
3) The defenders mark tightly to win possession.
5) Only 2 defenders play with the support player.

Exercise n. 188

Players
9 + 1 goalkeeper.

Duration
Six 5 minute sessions. Change of positions every 5 minutes.

Objectives
Tactical play for first exchanges and runs by the attacking players to take diagonal shots.

Description
Group 4A dribbles the ball and plays 1-2 combinations to attack the goal defended by group 5B and the goalkeeper. Group A has a playmaker who moves inside a 15-meter area to assist play with 1-2 combinations and dribbling. Group B plays with two sweepers and three players who mark their opponents. The shot has to be hit in under 2 minutes from outside the area. Another group alternates with group A every 2 minutes.

Variations
1) Alternate the roles of the groups with 5 attacking players and 4 defenders.
2) The support player is marked in the central area.
3) Two goalkeepers who can only use their feet.

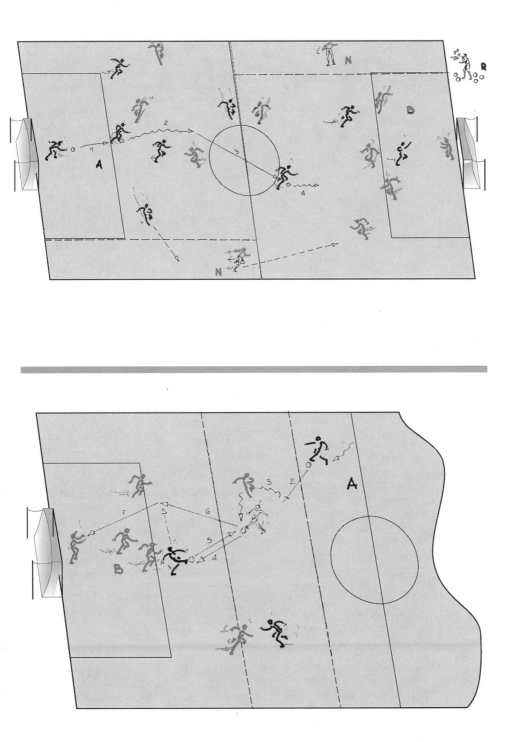

Exercise n. 189

Players
6 + 1 goalkeeper.

Duration
Five 5 minute sessions. Change of positions every 5 minutes.

Objectives
Exercise based on the playmaker for the position of the play and the shot from a distance.

Description
Group 3A plays two-touch soccer to attack the goal defended by group 3B and the goalkeeper. Group A has a playmaker who plays in the 10-meter area and assists the play with fast exchanges and dribbling. Only the playmaker can shoot and he must take his shot in under 1 minute.

Variations
1) If group B gains possession the roles are quickly inverted.
2) A support player in the 10-meter area only to play long passes.
3) Man to man marking.

Exercise n. 190

Players
16 + 2 support players.

Duration
15/20 minutes.

Objectives
1) Alternation of the play between one field and the other for rapid attacking and defensive moves.
2) Tactical play for dribbling, fast exchanges and 1-2 combinations.

Description
Groups 4C and 4D play each other for possession with various combinations and 1-2's to attack the regular goal defended by the goalkeeper. The two groups alternate between attack and defense. Groups 4A and 4B carry out the same exercise in area **2**. At R's signal the group in possession in each area passes the ball to the support player in the central area. The support player plays it on into the opposite area. The group that gains possession attacks the goal in its own area which is defended by the other group.

Variations
1) The support player in possession can move into play as a playmaker.
2) The support players in the central area pass the ball to the wings.

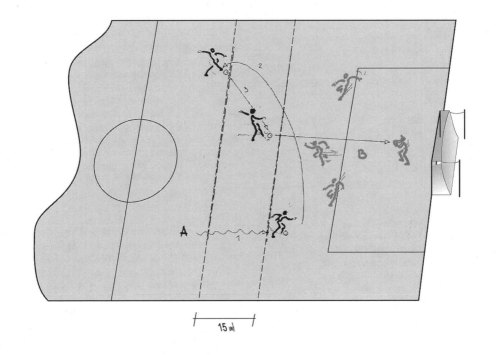

15 m

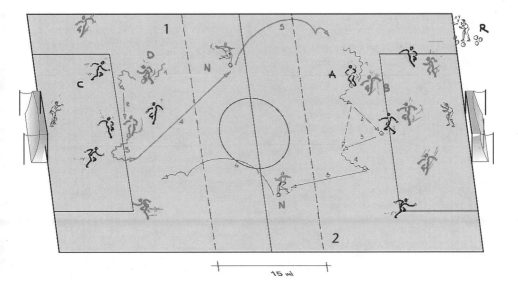

15 m

Exercise n. 191

Players
6.

Duration
10/12 minutes. Change of positions between players every minute.

Objectives
1) Fast reaction of the attacking player to dribble free of the two defenders.
2) Fast control of the ball and rapid finish.

Description
In a limited area of the field groups A-B-C and D-E-F are positioned in a triangle. They play straight, first time passes to each other (15/20 meters). At R's signal the player in possession from each group attacks the 3 meter goal on the other side of the field, (B attacks goal no **1**. and is marked by players E and F of the other group and D attacks goal no **2**. and is marked by A and C of the other group).

Variations
1) If the defenders gain possession they have to finish in under 20 seconds on the goal defended by the attacking player and goal-keeper.
2) At R's signal an attacking player comes in from off the field to play 1-2 combinations and quick shots at goal.

Exercise n. 192

Players
6 + 1 goalkeeper.

Duration
8/10 three minute sessions.

Description
Group 3A attacks the 5-meter goal defended by the goalkeeper and group 3B. In the 10-meter area **1** a player from group A lays fast passes on.

Variations
1) Shot hit after a 1-2 combinations.
2) Only the playmaker shoots at goal.
3) If group B gains possession the roles are inverted.

Objectives
1) Dribbling of the ball and tight marking.
2) The playmaker in the central area builds up the play with fast exchanges.

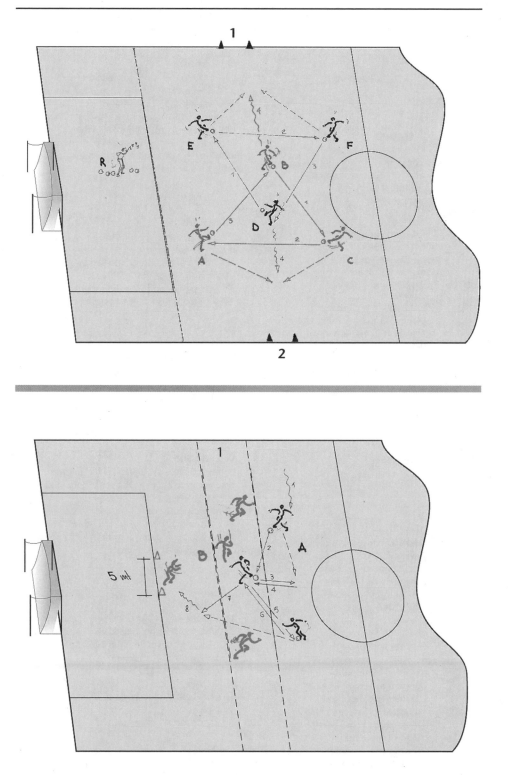

Exercise n. 193

Players
18 + 2 goalkeepers.

Duration
Five 5 minute sessions. The defenders and the attacking players change positions every 5 minutes.

Objectives
1) Tactical move for attacking players who have the numerical advantage to develop fast attacking moves.
2) Attacking players with a playmaker to get past the neutral area and movement of players in space.
3) The players move faster outside the 10-meter areas.

Description
Group 5A plays three-touch soccer to attack the goal defended by group 4B and the goalkeeper. The attacking players cannot enter the 10-meter wide area with the ball. At the same time in area **2** group 5B attacks the goal defended by group 4A and the goalkeeper. The attacking players cannot enter the 10-meter wide area with the ball.

Variations
1) A playmaker in the 10 meter area as a playmaker for the build-up.
2) Change of positions between an attacking player and a defender.
3) Long passes and first time shots at goal.
4) Dribbling of the ball and tight marking.

Exercise n. 194

Players
22 + 2 goalkeepers.

Duration
An attacking move every 2 minutes for 18/20 moves. Change of positions between attacking players and defenders every three moves.

Objectives
1) Tactical move which requires different tactics in each area of the field.
2) Primary use of the wings in area **2** to develop the attack and particular attention paid to the defense starting from the halfway line.

Description
Groups 11A and 11B play each other for possession to shoot at the goals defended by the goalkeepers. The groups in the central 40-meter area **2** play two-touch soccer and concentrate their game on the wings. The players in areas **1** and **3** move freely and can only finish with a header.

Variations
1) Exercise without goalkeepers (12 against 12 with the keepers outside the small area).
2) 2 support players in area **2** for dribbling of the ball and tight marking.
3) Individual tactics (1 against 1).
4) Limit touches.
5) 3 players from each group in area **2** for first time passes.

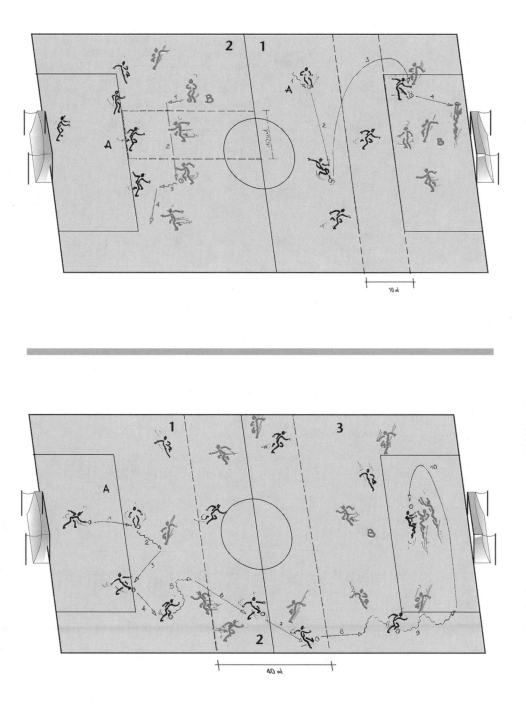

Exercise n. 195

Players
22 + 2 goalkeepers.

Duration
18/20 attacking moves. Finishing in under 2 minutes and change of positions between attacking players and defenders every 5 minutes.

Objectives
1) Tactical move for the build-up of fast moves and rapid finishing.
2) Perfection of individual technique.
3) The players play first time passes to each other in area **2**.

Description
Groups 11A and 11B play each other for possession to shoot at the goals defended by the goalkeepers. In the 40-meter area **2** the groups play 1-2 combinations and dribble the ball with a max. of 4 players. In areas **1** and **3** the players pass the ball to their teammates in area **2** from the center of the pitch. In areas **1** and **3** the players finish with diagonal shots.

Variations
1) Any combination in areas **1** and **3** and two-touch soccer in area **2**.
2) The groups build up the play from the center of the pitch.
3) A player acts as playmaker in areas **1** and **3**.
4) Finishing shot from designated player.

Exercise n. 196

Players
13 + 1 support player + 2 goalkeepers.

Duration
8/10 five minute sessions.

Objectives
1) Rapid movement of players and ball.
2) The game develops along the wings.

Description
Groups 6A and 7B play for possession to shoot at the goals defended by the goalkeepers. Group 6A plays three touch soccer with short diagonal passes and group 7B plays two-touch soccer with vertical and horizontal passes. The support player acts as playmaker.

Variations
1) 8 against 6 + 2 players.
2) One group plays to keep possession and move the ball around the field and the other to attack the two goals.
3) Change of tactical positions between players every 5 minutes.

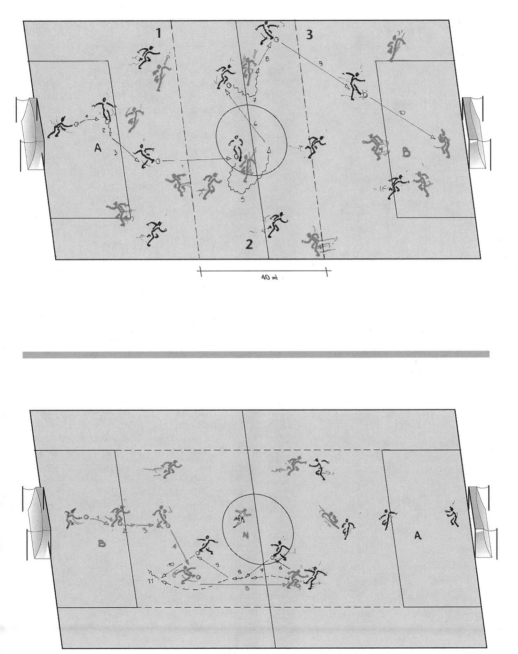

Exercise n. 197

Players
9 + 1 support player.

Duration
15 minutes.

Description
Groups 5A and 4B play each other to keep possession on a small pitch. The player in possession must enter into one of the 10 x 10 meter areas by dribbling the ball through a small goal. The support player outside the indicated areas assists the player in possession with first time passes.

Objectives
Improvement of dribbling techniques.

Variations
1) 5 against 5 + 2 support players.
2) 3 against 3 + 4 support players.
3) 3 support players can also play inside the indicated areas.

Exercise n. 198

Players
12 + 1 support player.

Duration
Six 5 minutes sessions.

Description
Group 7A plays two-touch soccer to attack the small 3-meter goals on the halfway line which are defended by the goalkeeper and group 5B. When group 5B gains possession they must carry it into one of the areas indicated by the dotted lines and all the players must pass the halfway line. The support player assists the play with 1-2 combinations, first time passes and dribbling of the ball.

Objectives
Group 7A must use the entire field and keep the play flowing.

Variations
1) Group 7A must play two 1-2 combinations before finishing.
2) Group 5B must play two touches to carry the ball into another area.
3) The support player shoots first time at the small goals.

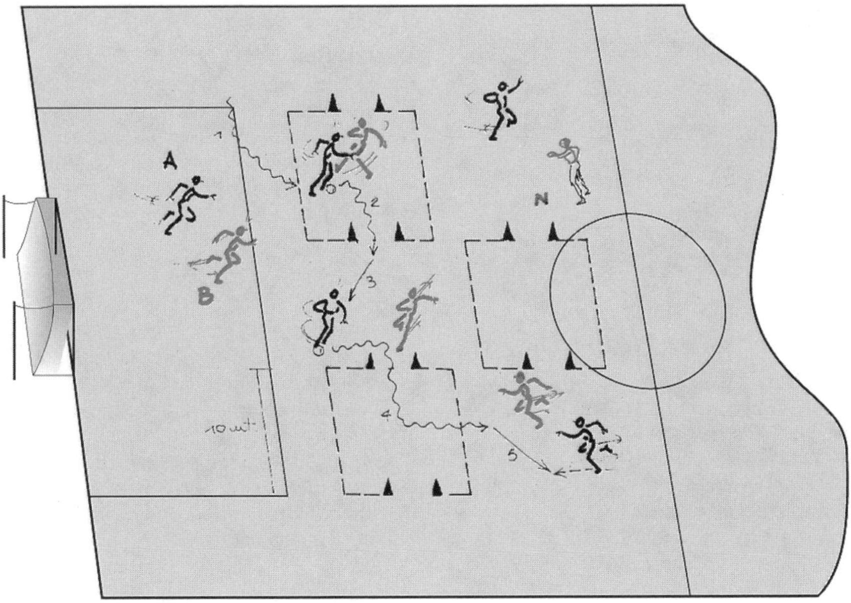
A
B
N
1
2
3
4
5
10 mt.

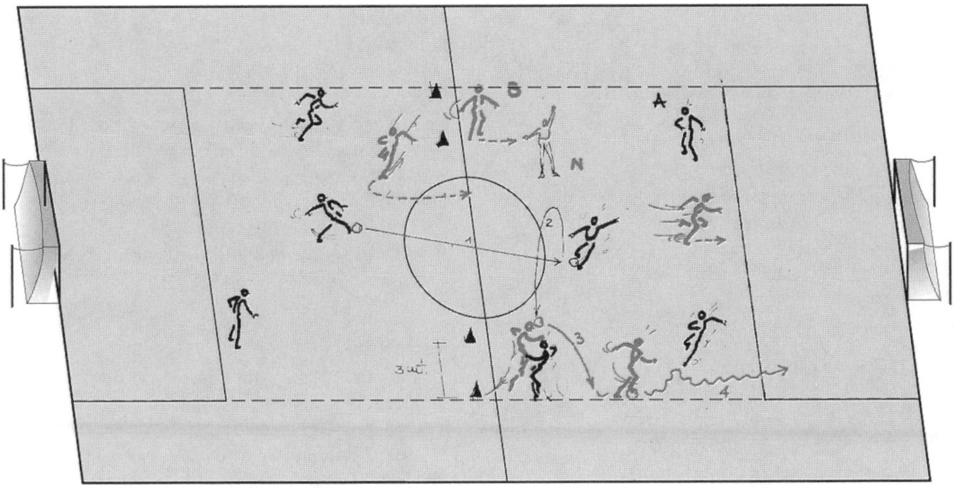
A
B
N
1
2
3
4
3 mt.

Exercise n. 199

Players
14.

Duration
8/10 attacking moves per group.

Objectives
1) Attacking play in both directions with a playmaker who assists the play with fast exchanges and 1-2 combinations.
2) Tactical move to speed up attacking moves and increase aggression in defense.

Description
Group 4A passes the halfway line to attack the 6 meter goals defended by group 3B and the two goalkeepers who can use their feet. Group 4A plays three-touch soccer. Group A must shoot and attack the goal defended by group C in under 1 minute.

Variations
1) The attacking group must play three 1-2 combinations before shooting.
2) Time limit for the shot for the group with the numerical advantage.
3) Change of positions between attacking players and defenders every 3 minutes.
4) 6 attacking players and 3 defenders. The attacking players must finish in under 30 seconds.

Exercise n. 200

Players
18 + 2 goalkeepers.

Duration
8/10 three minute sessions.

Objectives
Tactical move for attacking players who are in numerical advantage to give the move greater speed and intensity.

Description
Group 4A plays in area **1** with three players, one of whom stays on the left wing. They play two-touch soccer and attack the goal defended by group 5B and the goalkeeper. Group 4B plays in area **2** with three player's one of whom stays on the right wing. It attacks the goal defended by group 5A and the goalkeeper. The players on the wings assist the play with long, high crosses for finishing headers.

Variations
1) If the defenders gain possession they must maintain possession for 1 minute and play at least three 1-2 combinations.
2) A designated attacking player shoots from a distance.
3) An attacking player acts as playmaker.
4) The attacking players change position with the defense every three minutes.
5) A support player plays with the group that doesn't have the ball.

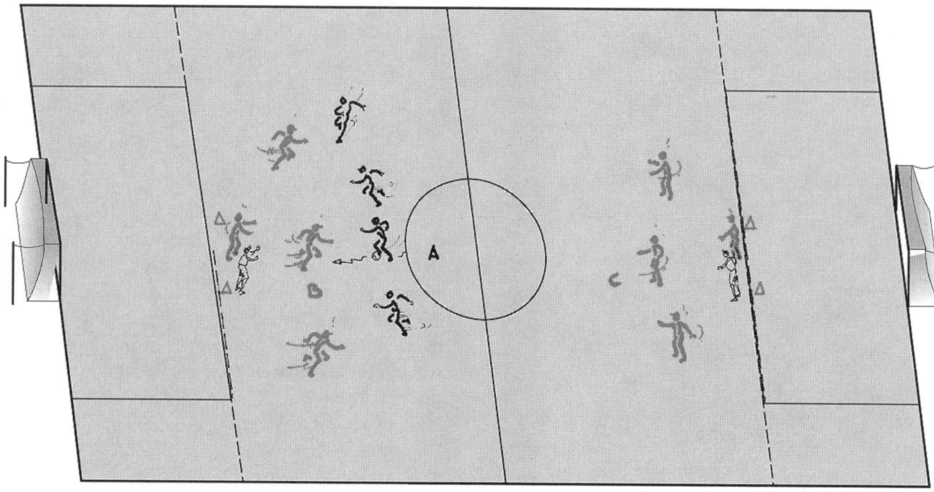
A
B
C

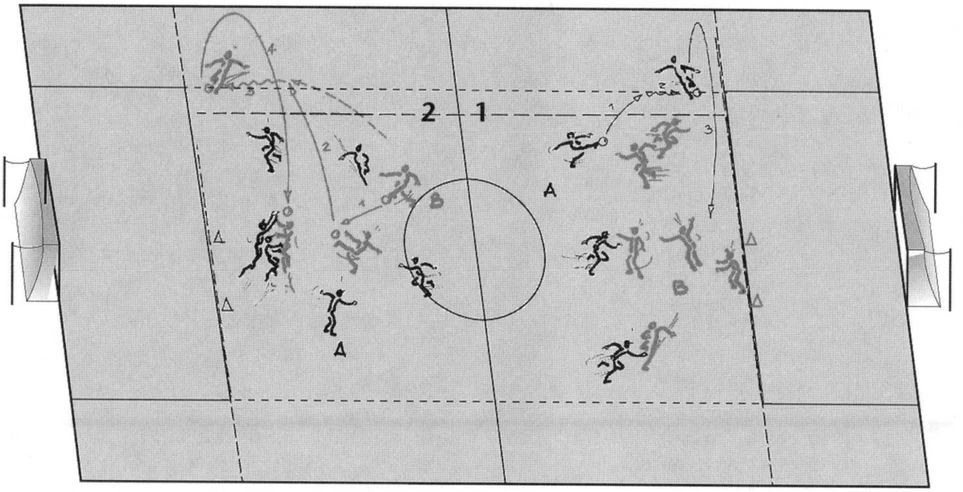
2
1
A
B

Exercise n. 201

Players
15 + 2 support players + 1 goalkeeper.

Duration
5/6 six minute sessions.

Objectives
1) Specific tactics for team-play in defense and in attack.
2) Fast attacking move from one smaller area to another bigger area.

Description
Group 4A plays to maintain possession and defend the small 3-meter goals in area **1**. Group 3B plays 1-2 combinations and dribbles the ball to attack the same goals. The support player plays first time passes when playing with group B. Groups 4A and 4B play three-touch soccer in area **2**. The two support players play with the group in possession attacking the 5-meter goal defended by the other group and the goalkeeper. The two neutral players assist dribbling of the ball. At R's signal all the players from area **1** attack the goal in area **2** which is defended by the goalkeeper and the other ten players. The attacking group must finish in under 1 minute.

Variations
1) No restrictions in areas **1** and **2**.
2) The support players play first time passes in area **2**.
3) At R's signal a support player from area **2** plays in goal but can only use his feet.

Exercise n. 202

Players
11 + 1 support player + 2 goalkeepers.

Duration
25 minutes. The defenders and the attacking players change their positions every 3 minutes.

Objectives
The attacking players exchange passes rapidly, they must concentrate on first time passes of the ball.

Description
In area **1** group 3A must dribble the ball across a 20-meter area defended by group 3B and a goalkeeper who cannot touch the ball with his hands. When the defenders gain possession or at R's signal they play the ball to the support player in the central area of the pitch. The support player plays the ball on to the attacking players of the same group in the opposite area. Group 2A and a goalkeeper defend in area **2**.

Variations
1) Alternate attacking players and defenders.
2) Two players defend the 20 meter areas, alternating with the defending group.
3) The attacking group must play at least two 1-2 combinations before finishing in under 30 seconds beyond the 20 meter area.

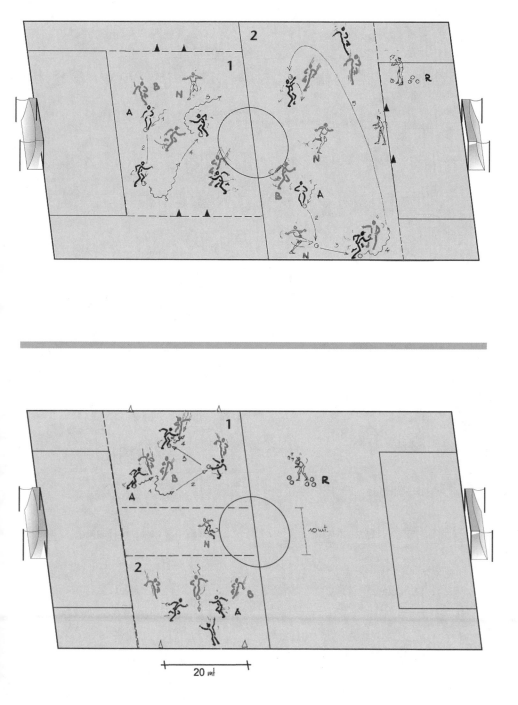

Exercise n. 203

Players
16.

Duration
25 minutes. Change of positions between players every 5 minutes.

Objectives
Alternation of attacking and defensive moves for a development of specific characteristics.

Description
Groups A and B play each other for possession to attack the 2-meter goals in areas **1**, **2**, **3** and **4**. At R's signal the players from group A in areas **1** and **2** unite and move into area **5** to defend the two goals on the sidelines. The players from group B playing in areas **3** and **4** unite to attack the goals defended by group A. The players from group A playing in areas **3** and **4** unite with the goalkeeper to defend the goal in area **6**. The players from group B playing in area **1** and **2** attack the goal in area **6**. The ball in area **5** is carried by a player from group B while the ball in area **6** is played by one of the players from group A.

Variations
1) In area **5** the game is played with limited touches.
2) In area **6** the shot is hit after the group has played three 1-2 combinations.
3) The ball is played by R to a support player who acts as a playmaker in areas **5** and **6**.

Exercise n. 204

Players
10 + 1 support player + 2 goalkeepers.

Duration
7/8 three minute sessions. The attacking players and defenders change positions every three minutes.

Objectives
Tactical play based on the playmaker who creates fast exchanges.

Description
Group 3A plays two-touch soccer to attack the goal defended by group 2B and the goalkeeper in area **1**. One of the players from group A acts as playmaker. The same exercise is practiced in area **2** with group 3B attacking and group 2A defending. Both groups are assisted by a support player who plays first time passes and long crosses from the central 18 meter areas of the pitch to each group in his own area.

Variations
1) The playmaker cannot shoot.
2) The two goals may be higher and narrower (as for olympic handball).

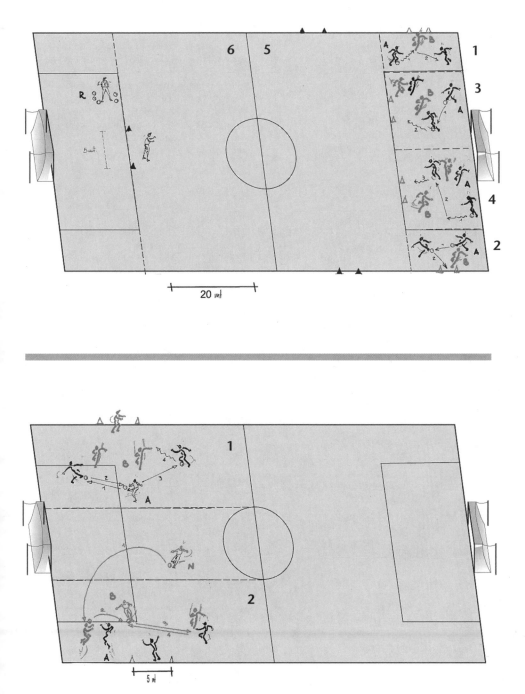

Exercise n. 205

Players
12.

Duration
Move the ball from one area to the other every 2 minutes, 8/10 times.

Objectives
Tactical move to develop fast attacking and defensive moves.

Description
Group 3B plays three-touch soccer to attack the three meter goal defended by group 2A and the goalkeeper in area 1. Group 3A plays two-touch soccer in area 2 to attack the goal defended by group 2B. At R's signal the defenders pass the ball to their teammates who are inside the 3 meter area in area 3. They play the ball to their attacking teammates in areas 1 and 2 to continue the attack.

Variations
1) The player in area 2 moves in to play with the ball to play 4 against 2.
2) On the pass from the player in area 3 the positions change (2 attack and 3 defend).
3) 1 support player in area 1 and 1 in area 2 as playmakers. No restrictions.

Exercise n. 206

Players
12 + 1 support player.

Duration
Six 5 minute sessions. The defenders and the attacking players change positions every 5 minutes.

Objectives
Change of position and fast moves between players and the ball.

Description
In area 1 the players from group 2A must take the ball across a 20-meter area which is defended by the players from group 2B and two goalkeepers who can only use their feet. The same exercise is carried out in area 2 with group 2B attacking and group 2A defending. The support player in the 10-meter central area assists play with long passes.

Variations
1) The support player moves out of the 10-meter area to play as an attacking player in areas 1 and 2.
2) The two goalkeepers only play first time passes.
3) The support player in the central area plays as a playmaker.
4) At R's signal the ball is passed from one area to the other.

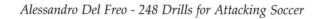

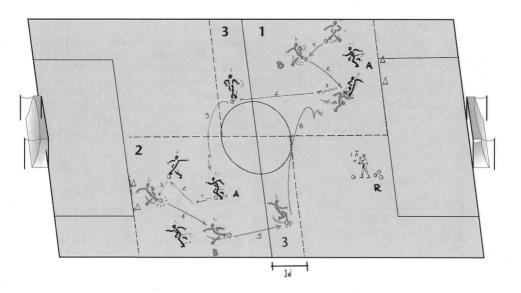

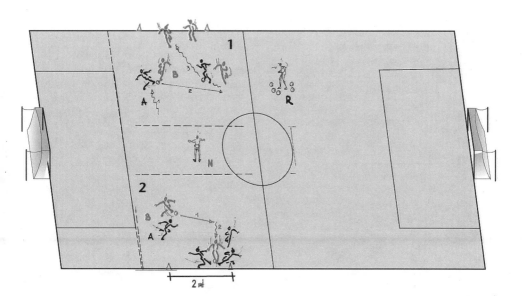

Exercise n. 207

Players
10 + 1 goalkeeper.

Duration
Six 5 minute sessions.

Objectives
Tactical move to get players used to rapid change in attacking and defensive play.

Description
Group 6A plays three-touch soccer against group 4B which plays without any restrictions in the midfield area. Group A defends the small 3-meter goals placed at the corners of the pitch and attacks the regular goal. Group B defends the regular goal and attacks the small goals.

Variations
1) Group B defends the regular goal and two of the small ones.
2) Group A designates one of its players to shoot before each move.
3) Groups B alternates the attack on one designated goal for each attacking move.

Exercise n. 208

Players
8 + 1 support player.

Duration
Six 5 minute sessions.

Description
Group 2A defends and group 2B attacks in area **1**. Group 2B defends and group 2A attacks in area **2**. The objective of the exercise is to take the ball across the 10-meter area on the side of the pitch. At R's signal the defending group with the ball passes it to a support player in a 10-meter area. The support player plays a high ball to the players of the same group in the opposite area to finish. R speeds up the change from area to area.

Objectives
Tactical move for possession from the defenders and the pass to the support player to the attacking move.

Variations
1) The support player takes the ball across the area on a run having played a couple of 1-2 combinations.
2) He runs left foot passes to area **2** and right foot passes to area **1**.

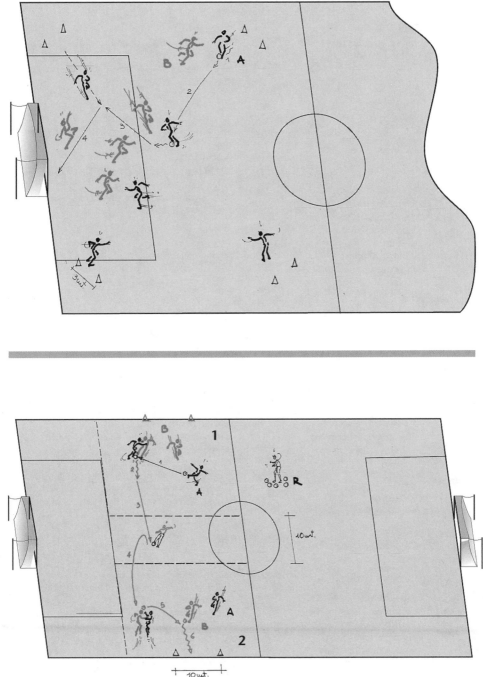

Exercise n. 209

Players
14 + 1 support player
+ 2 goalkeepers.

Duration
3 ten minute sessions.

Objectives
1) Move to improve the game through passes and fast runs.
2) Tactical phase to improve vision in attack.

Description
Groups 7A and 7B defend a regular goal and two 3-meter goals each in their own half. The support player plays long passes to speed up the attack.

Variations
1) One group attacks the regular goals and the other group attacks the 4 small goals.
2) 8 players defend the small goals and 6 players defend the regular goals.

Exercise n. 210

Players
10 + 2 support players
+ 2 goalkeepers.

Duration
Five 6 minute sessions.

Objectives
Fast move based on the 2 support players who act as playmakers in defense and in attack.

Description
Groups 5A and 5B play each other for possession with the help of two neutral players. The two neutral players dribble the ball and mark tightly. In each half 3 defenders tackle 2 attacking players from the other group assisted by two support players.

Variations
1) The two support players play with the team in possession only.
2) Only the support players can shoot.
3) During play an attacking player changes positions with a defending player.

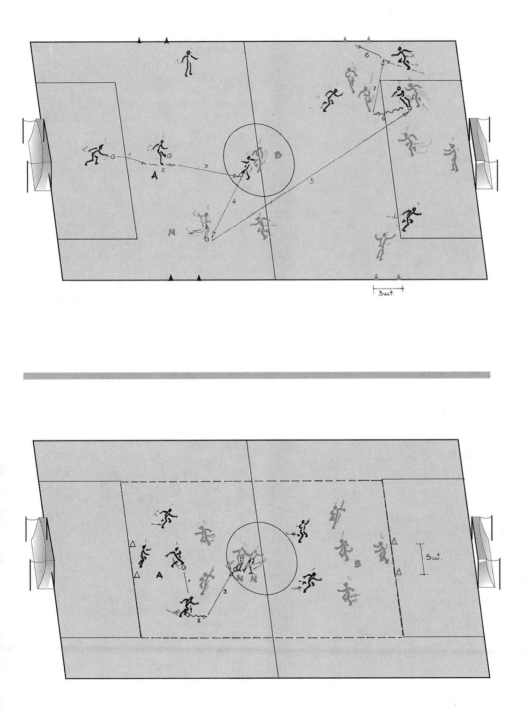

Exercise n. 211

Players
12 + 2 support players

Duration
Two 10 minute sessions.

Description
First Exercise - In area **1** groups 6A and 6B play three-touch soccer to attack the small 5-meter goals.

Second Exercise - In areas **1** and **2** the two teams play four-touch soccer to attack the 5-meter goals.

Third Exercise - The two teams play on a regular pitch to attack the regular goals. They are assisted by two support players who play with the team in possession.

Objectives
1) Technical and tactical play for collective attacking move.
2) Improvement of exchanges through fast passes.

Variations
1) Change the direction of play.
2) Alternate dribbling of the ball with 1-2 combinations.
3) The support players shoot from outside the area.

Exercise n. 212

Players
15 + 2 support players + 2 goalkeepers.

Description
Group 7A attacks the regular goals and the small 2-meter goals on a regular pitch. Group 8A plays two-touch soccer to defend the four goals and keep possession. The two support players assist play with first time passes and direct the offensive and defensive moves.

Duration
15/20 minutes. Change of position between the two groups every 5 minutes.

Objectives
Alternation between attacking and defensive moves for basic tactics.

Variations
1) At R's signal the two support players play with one group only.
2) Limited touches.
3) At R's signal a defender joins the attack.

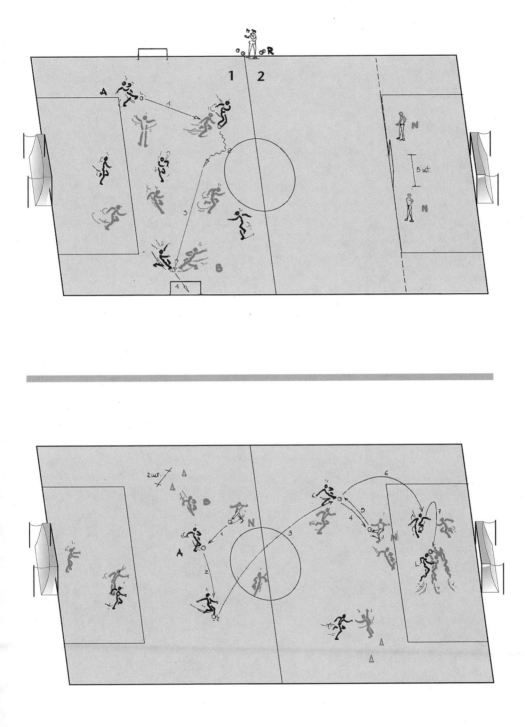

Exercise n. 213

Players
12 + 2 goalkeepers.

Duration
Eight 3 minute sessions.

Objectives
Development of tactical and technical moves for the striker.

Description
Groups 4A and 4B play each other to attack the small goals in area **1**. At R's signal the group in possession passes it into area **2** to its teammates 2A and 2B who play each other to attack the small goals in under 30 seconds.

Variations
1) In area **1**, 4 against 3 or 5 against 4 + 2 support players.
2) In area **2** dribbling of the ball before the shot.

Exercise n. 214

Players
12 + 2 support players.

Duration
15/20 minutes.

Objectives
The two support players speed up the play with short first time passes and 1-2 combinations in small spaces.

Description
Groups 6A and 6b play each other for possession on a small pitch. Group A defends the small 5-meter goals **1** and group B defends goals **2**. Both groups must finish in under 1 minute.

Variations
1) First time shots at goal.
2) The two groups only play long passes to the support players.
3) Two passes and shot.
4) Only the support players can shoot.
5) At R's signal one player moves from one group to the other.

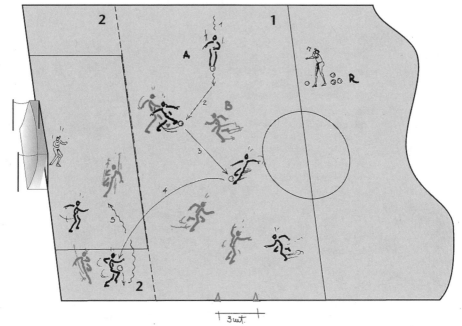

Exercise n. 215

Players
10 + 2 support players.

Duration
Five 5 minute sessions.

Objectives
Fast vision of play while freeing oneself of a marking player.

Description
Groups 5A and 5B play each other to attack three small 2-meter goals placed in a semi-circle on a small pitch. Group B plays first time passes to attack and many combinations to defend and group A dribbles the ball when attacking and marks tightly in defense. The support players assist the play with short passes.

Variations
1) One group defends the three goals and the other attacks.
2) 4 against 4 + 1 support player.
3) One group attacks the central goal and the other the two lateral ones.

Exercise n. 216

Players
16 + 2 goalkeepers.

Duration
Five 5 minute sessions.

Description
Group 4B defends and group 2A attacks in area **1**, group 4A defends and group 2B attacks in area **2**. The two groups are assisted only in their attacking moves by two of their teammates from outside the field. The move builds up in under 1 minute from the defenders to the attacking players in the other half of the field. The players cannot move into the central 10-meter area with the ball, only the two goalkeepers defend the six meter goals in this area.

Objectives
Tactical play for teamwork and efficiency of players.

Variations
1) The two attacking players dribble the ball.
2) A support player plays in the central area as a playmaker.
3) The player off the pitch can move into play if he is in possession but he must be immediately substituted by a teammate.

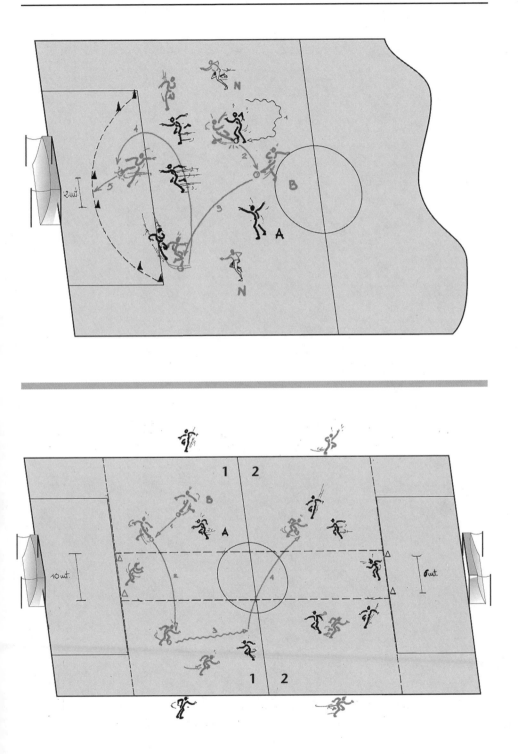

CHAPTER FIVE

Tactical moves for fast counter-attacks

1) Fast solutions in counter-attack from openings and wide balls on both wings.
2) Perfection of collective tactics and organizational formations in counter-attack.

The exercises are of a more technical nature in this chapter. They are responsible for the perfection of motor activities in certain situations which require a more specific technique. The counter-attack is in effect a phase of the game which is loved by the spectators and players alike especially for the freedom of movement it allows.

Since the counter-attack can occur at any moment during the game when the opponents lose possession and the attack is in numerical advantage a correct preparation for this phase of the game is essential.

Exercise that make the move flow from a physical and mental aspect are fundamental.

The players will be trained to perform technical and tactical moves of the highest quality.

Individual play and teamwork are both essential for an effective counter-attack. The trainer will make considerations regarding both of these aspects in order to consolidate them and therefore achieve the ultimate performance for the players.

Exercise n. 217

Players
10 + 1 support players.

Duration
20 minutes. Change of the support player and of the two groups every five minutes.

Objectives
1) Tactical move to make the team without possession react as quickly as possible to regain the ball.
2) The attacking group builds up the attack along the wings.

Description
In a 16 x 60 m. area groups 5A and 5B play for possession. At R's signal the group in possession moves out of the area and plays two-touch soccer and long passes to attack the two small 5-meter goals on the halfway line. The two goals are defended by the other group. If the defending team gains possession it passes the ball to the support player who directs the attack on the two small goals with the new group that plays two-touch soccer.

Variations
1) At R's signal the group in possession passes it to the support player who, from the small area, plays it on to the group attacking the small goal.
2) If the defenders gain possession during the attack on the small goals, they immediately move in to attack the regular goals defended by the other group.

Exercise n. 218

Players
16 + 2 goalkeepers.

Duration
Five 5 minute sessions.

Objectives
Tactical play for teamwork and efficiency of players.

Description
The support player passes to a player from group 3B from the corner. The attacking player is on the right hand corner of the penalty area, with his group he starts the attack on the goal defended by the goalkeeper and group 6A. The attacking group has to finish in under 30 seconds. If group 6A gains possession it attacks the three small goals on the halfway line with three players. These goals are defended by group 3B and group 1A (5 attacking players against 4 defenders).

Variations
1) The two attacking players dribble the ball.
2) A support player plays in the central area as playmaker.
3) The player off the pitch can move into play if he is in possession by he must be immediately substituted by a teammate.

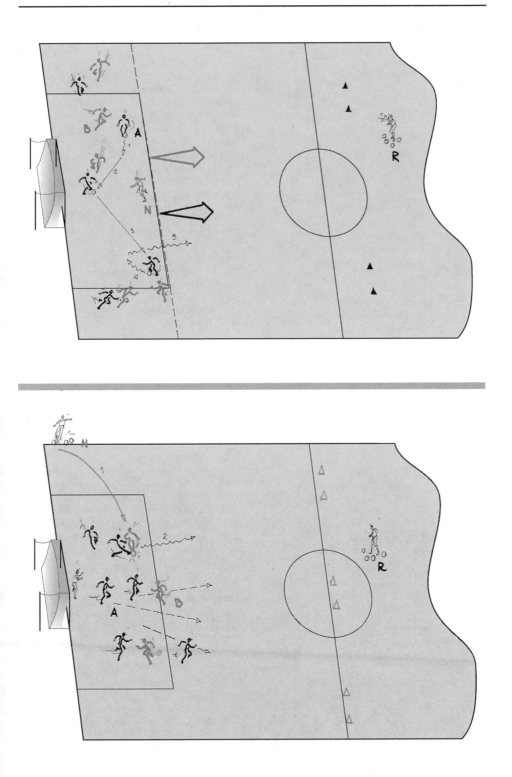

Exercise n. 219

Players
9 + 1 goalkeeper.

Duration
25/30 moves. Every three attacking moves group C is substituted by another group.

Objectives
1) Tactical move to change the play from a small area to a larger one.
2) Fast move to allow the designated player to finish rapidly.

Description
Groups 3A and 3B play each other for possession in the 10 meter area **1**. At R's signal the group in possession attacks the goal defended by group 3C and the goalkeeper and must finish in under 30 seconds. The attacking group builds up the attack sending one player into each of the areas indicated **2**, **3** and **4** until the edge of the penalty area. All players move freely once inside the area. In the meantime the group left in area **1** starts a new move with group D.

Variations
1) Attack only from the wings.
2) 3 + 3 + 1 support player.
3) The attacking group has one player who plays freely and the other who plays two-touch soccer.

Exercise n. 220

Players
6 + 2 support players + 1 goalkeeper.

Duration
25/30 shots from the support players in succession from the two corners.

Objectives
1) Tactical move for attacking move on the break.
2) Possibilities of creating finishing chances for all players.

Description
The support player plays a high ball in from the corner. The keeper moves to punch out to the two groups which stand 30 meters from the goal. The group that wins possession moves to attack the goal which is defended by the other group. The support players alternate their corners after every attacking move.

Variations
1) Limit touches and finish in under 1 minute.
2) The support player who hasn't taken the corner joins in the attack from the wing.
3) All three attacking players must touch the ball before the shot.

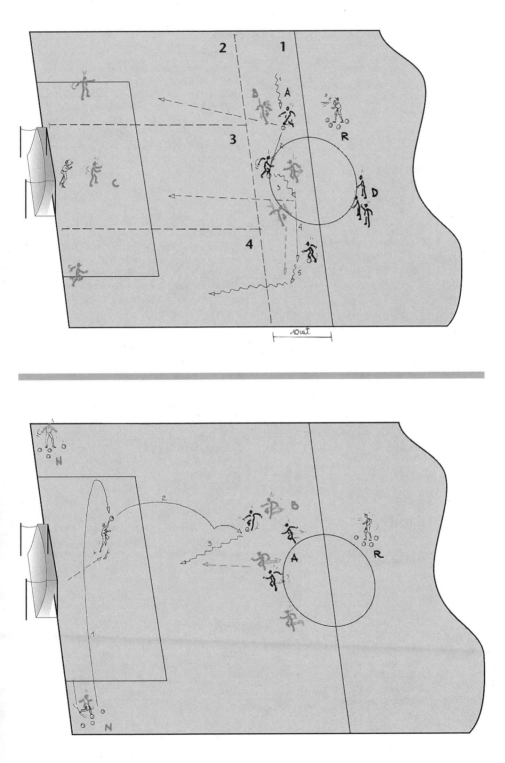

Exercise n. 221

Players
6 + 2 support players.

Duration
25/30 corner kicks. After each move groups A and B change positions.

Objectives
Co-ordinated technique and tactical play for the build-up in the attacking move.

Description
The support player takes the corner for group 3A which builds up the attack on the goal defended by the goalkeeper with a 1-2 combination. When the corner is taken group 3B moves into play to defend the goal. If group B gains possession it immediately attacks the two small goals on the halfway line which are defended by group A and the two support players who move along the wings.

Variations
1) When the defenders gain possession they attack the other goals which are defended by two players from the other group.
2) Only one designated player can shoot from among the three attacking players.

Exercise n. 222

Players
8.

Duration
15/20 minutes. Change of position between players every three minutes.

Objectives
1) Possibility of making the most of every advantage situation.
2) Co-ordination of individual and team moves for organized tactical play.

Description
Groups 4A and 4B play each other on a small pitch. They attack the small goals in the opposite area and have to pass the ball from one area to the other across a 20-meter space in the center of the field. Only two designated players from the two groups can shoot, another acts as playmaker and the other assists the move without going beyond the halfway line.

Variations
1) The group in possession plays first time balls once it has passed the 20-meter area.
2) Diagonal shots to finish.
3) The attacking group plays 4 against 3 after passing the 20-meter area.

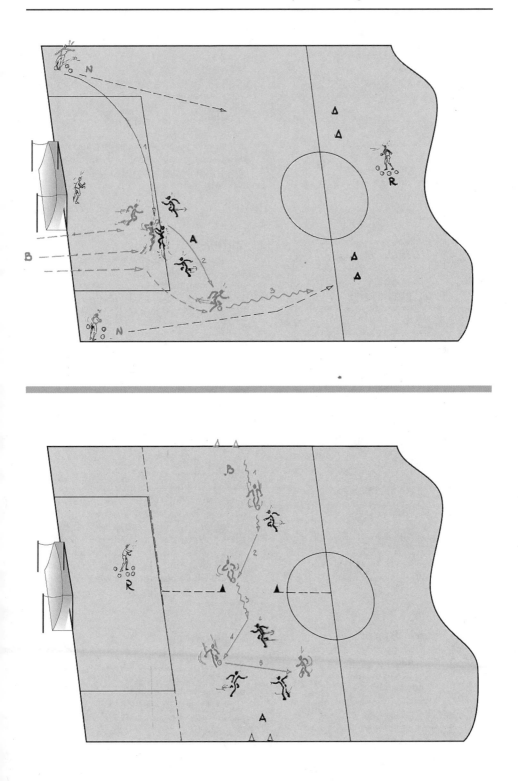

Exercise n. 223

Players
8 + 2 support players.

Duration
15/20 minutes. R speeds up the attack by alternating the attack of the two groups every 2 minutes.

Objectives
1) Intensive play and players dribble the ball to move.
2) Change of play to develop rapid attacking moves.

Description
In area **1** groups 4A and 4b dribble the ball and play 1-2 combinations when attacking and mark tightly when defending. At R's signal group B attacks the goal in area **2** defended by the goalkeeper and group A. The group in attack must cross a 15-meter area and before the shot all the players must touch the ball. In area **3** the exercise is repeated from the beginning with the roles inverted.

Variations
1) 4 against 4 + 1 support player who starts the attack at R's signal.
2) The attacking group plays first time passes.
3) At R's signal the player in possession attacks the goal defended by two defenders.

Exercise n. 224

Players
6 + 1 support player + 1 goalkeeper.

Duration
15/20 minutes. Attacking move every minute.

Objectives
1) Tactical move for fast opening on the break.
2) Tactical move to improve vision in attack.

Description
The support player takes the corner for group 3A which builds up the attack on the goal defended by the goalkeeper with a 1-2 combination. When the corner is taken group 3B moves into play to defend the goal. If group B gains possession it immediately attacks the two small goals on the halfway line which are defended by group A and the two support players who move along the wings.

Variations
1) A player from each group dribbles the ball, the others play three-touch soccer.
2) Only the player played on by the support player is allowed to shoot.
3) The player in possession plays first time passes and is not attacked by any player from either group.

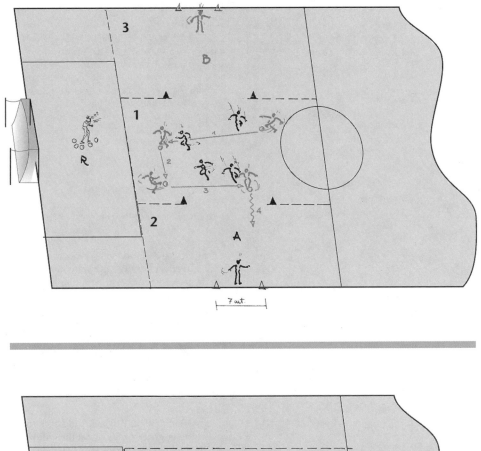

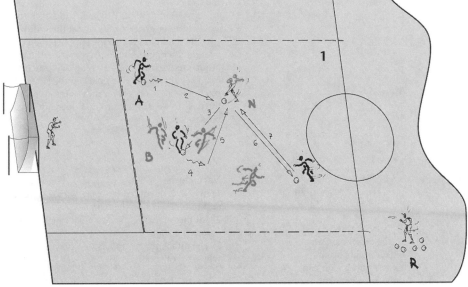

Exercise n. 225

Players
8 + 1 support players + 1 goalkeeper.

Duration
15/20 minutes. R alternates the two groups every two minutes to build up the attack.

Objectives
Tactical move for attacking play along the wings.

Description
Groups 4A and 4B play each other for possession in area **1**. At R's signal the group in possession plays the ball across a 20-meter area to the support player outside the pitch. The support player plays a relatively long pass down the wing to start a fast attacking move. The group that gains possession attacks the goal defended by the goalkeeper and the other group.

Variations
1) The player who gains possession on the wing must move out to shoot from the center of the penalty area.
2) Attack on goal in under 30 seconds.
3) All players in the attacking team must move into the penalty area before shooting.

Exercise n. 226

Players
10 + 1 support players.

Duration
15/20 minutes.

Objectives
1) In area **2** the group in possession attacks the goal on the break.
2) Tactical move based on the attacking game which builds up in areas **1** and **2** with continuous movement of the players.

Description
Groups 5A and 5B play in area **1** to attack the 2 small 3-meter goals. At R's signal the group with the ball passes it to the support player outside the pitch. All the players from the two groups move into area **2** to play two-touch soccer. They attack the two goals on the side of the pitch. The support player moves into play after the pass to assist the team that does not have possession.

Variations
1) In area **2** the defenders play with a sweeper and two players on the wings.
2) All the attacking players must touch the ball before the shot.
3) The attacking group has two playmakers who cannot shoot.

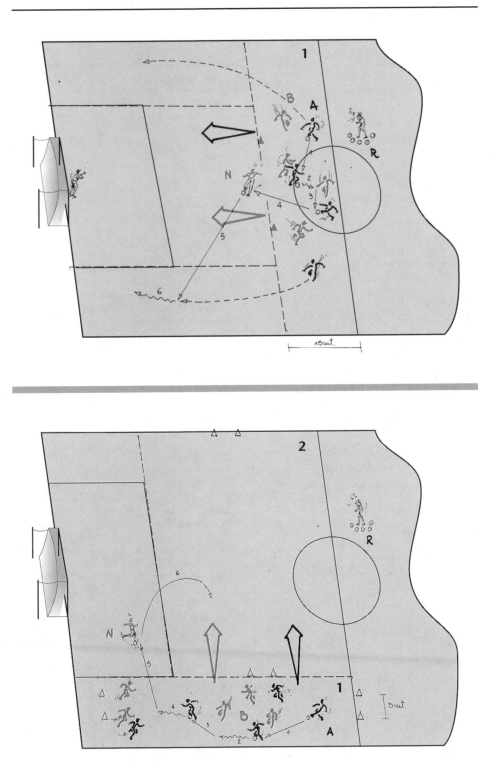

Exercise n. 227

Players
12 + 2 support players
+ 2 goalkeepers.

Description
In areas **1** and **2** groups 3A and 3B dribble the ball and mark tightly. At R's signal the team in possession moves out of the rectangle to attack the regular goal which is defended by the other group and the goalkeeper. The support player plays with the team that doesn't have the ball.

Duration
15/20 minutes.

Objectives
Fast move from a small area to a large one to force players to finish rapidly.

Variations
1) R alternates the group in attack every 2 minutes.
2) 4 against 4 plus 2 defenders on the edge of the box.
3) Only dribbling of the ball and 1-2 combinations inside the penalty area.
4) At R's signal the two groups in the two rectangles join to play 7 against 7 to attack and defend one single goal.

Exercise n. 228

Players
10 + 1 support player
+ 2 goalkeepers.

Description
A defender from group A and two attacking players from group B play each other in area **1**. In area **2** group 2A attacks and group 1B defends. In the central 10 meter area group 2A plays group 2B with a support player who dribbles the ball and marks tightly. R delivers the ball and the group that gains possession in the central area passes it to its attacking teammates who have to finish in under thirty seconds.

Duration
20 minutes. At R's signal the players in the central area alternate their passes to the two areas for the finish.

Objectives
Players in central area to gain possession and play the ball on for their teammates.

Variations
1) The support player can play the ball to areas **1** and **2**.
2) 2 defenders and 2 attacking players in areas **1** and **2**.
3) 3 defenders and 2 attacking players plus 2 support players.

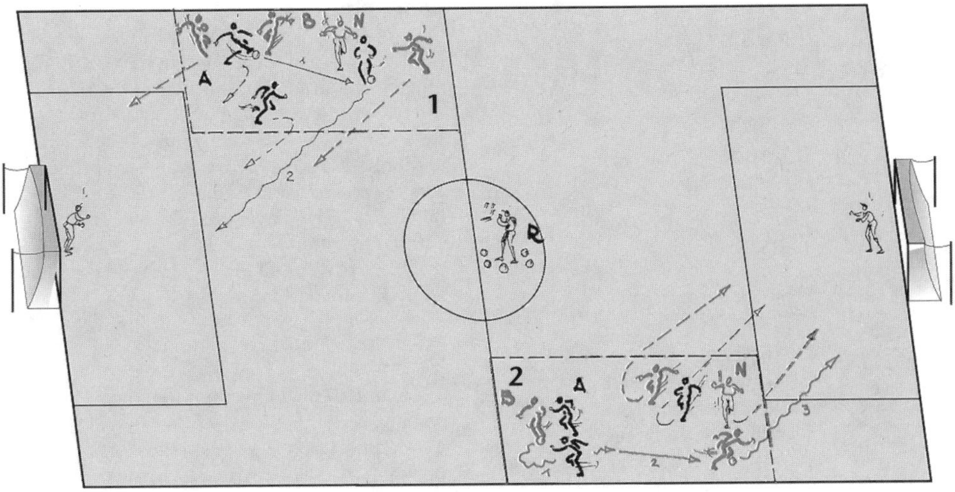
1
2
A
B
N
R

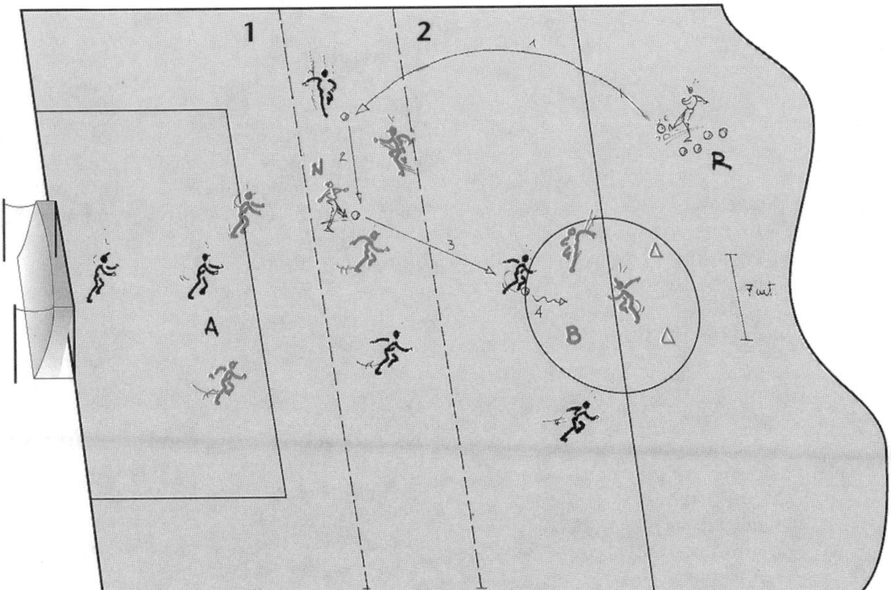
1
2
N
R
A
B
7 mt.
10 mt.

Exercise n. 229

Players
16 + 2 goalkeepers.

Duration
15/20 minutes.

Objectives
1) Vision of play based on the movement from a small area to a larger one.
2) Every two minutes R stimulates the attack outside the rectangles.

Description
Groups 4A and 4B dribble the ball and mark tightly. They play each other in the 40 x 20 rectangles on the sides of the pitch. At R's signal the player in the rectangle hits a long pass to the right wing on the other side of the pitch and only two players (one from each group A and B) can move out of the rectangle to win possession. The player with the ball must finish in under thirty seconds, he is marked by the other player and the regular goal is defended by the goalkeeper.

Variations
1) 2A and 2B play for possession outside the rectangles.
2) A support player plays on the edge of the penalty are to assist with first time passes.
3) The players outside the rectangle attack two 3-meter goals placed on the goal-lines.
4) The player who plays the long pass or other designated move moves out of the area to attack with the other player to play 2 against 1.

Exercise n. 230

Players
16 + 2 support players + 2 goalkeepers.

Duration
Five 5 minute sessions. The attacking players alternate with the defenders every five minutes of play.

Objectives
1) Build-up of constant movement of players and the ball.
2) Build-up of the attack on both sides of the field.

Description
Groups 8A and 8B play two-touch soccer for possession in area **1**. They attack the goals defended by the goalkeepers. When a group in possession enters into the lateral area **2** of the field it must attack the small 3-meter goals. The players in area **2** play each other and only the support players can move the play from area **1** to area **2**.

Variations

1) 7 against 7 with 4 support players. The support players have no restrictions on their play.
2) Limit touches in area **2** of the field.
3) The goalkeeper defends the two small goals.
4) The players in area **2** only dribble the ball.
5) Only the support players shoot at goal.

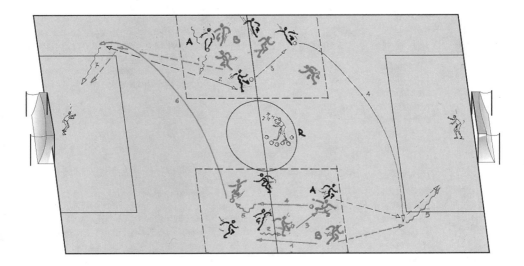

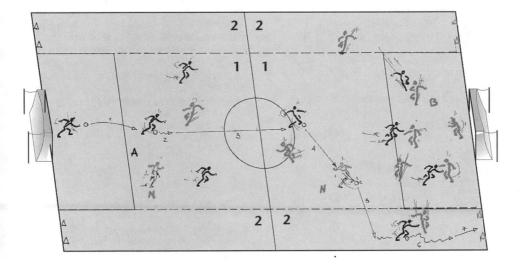

Exercise n. 231

Players
16.

Duration
An attacking move every 2 minutes.
10/12 moves.

Objectives
The group in possession uses an attacking tactical approach while the other group adopts a defensive strategy.

Description
Groups 6A and 6b play three-touch soccer for possession in the 40-meter area **1**. At R's signal the player with the ball passes it into area **2** where only two players play each other to win possession and finish. They are assisted by the two groups in area **1**.

Variations
1) A support player in area **2** to play the attacking group into the move.
2) At R's signal two players from area **1** move into area **2**.
3) The player with the ball in area **2** plays a long, high ball for his teammate's finishing header at goal.

Exercise n. 232

Players
10 + 2 support players + 2 goalkeepers.

Duration
15/20 minutes.

Objectives
Attack on the break for tactics in counter-attack.

Description
In the central 40-meter area groups 5A and 5B play for possession. At R's signal the player with the ball passes it to a support player who plays it on over the central area **1** to two players in area **2**. The player who gains possession attacks the goal which is defended by the goalkeeper and the other player.

Variations
1) The two support players with two balls pass into both areas of play at the same time.
2) Two designated players enter into area **2**.
3) Shots only from outside the box.

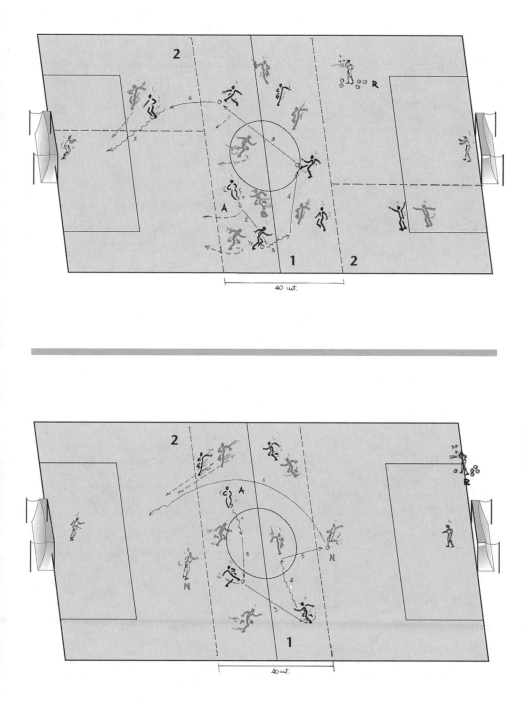

Exercise n. 233

Players
6 + 1 support player
+ 1 goalkeeper.

Duration
8/10 attacking moves
(1 every 2 minutes).

Description
Groups 3A and 3B and a support player play two-touch soccer in the 20 x 20 area **1**. At R's signal the support player kicks the ball into the wing in area **2** and two players (1 from each group) move to gain possession. The group in possession of the ball attacks the regular goal defended by the goalkeepers and by the other group.

Objectives
Rapid solution for moves on the break.

Variations
1) A sweeper as a defender at the center of the area.
2) Only a support player on the wing for the cross to the center of the area for a finishing header.
3) Only first-touch soccer in area **1**.

Exercise n. 234

Players
8 + 1 support player
+ 2 goalkeepers.

Duration
10/12 attacking moves
for each group.

Description
One half of the pitch is divided into areas **1** and **2**. Groups 4A and 4B play each other for possession. Group 4B attacks the goal in area **1** which is defended by a goalkeeper and group 4A. Group 4A attacks the goal in area **2** which is defended by a goalkeeper and group 4B. The game starts from the goalkeeper from group A's kickout to area **2** and the group that gains possession must finish in under one minute. The support player moves from one side of the pitch to the other for fast exchanges.

Objectives
1) Specific tactical maneuvers for fast finishes on goal.
2) Adaptation of players to quickly switch in counter-attacks.

Variations
1) 5 against 4 with one player assisting the play on the wings.
2) The support player assists the play only with long passes.
3) One group plays two-touch soccer, the other plays with no restrictions.

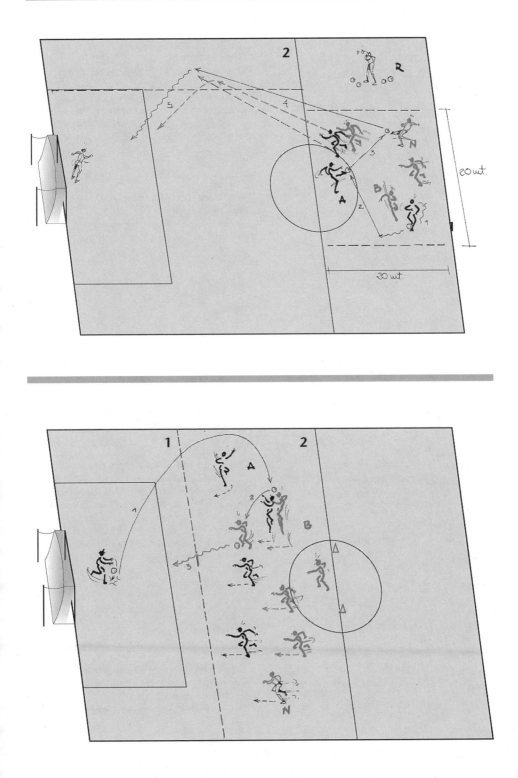

Exercise n. 235

Players
6 + 1 support player
+ 1 goalkeeper.

Description
Groups 3A and 3B dribble the ball in a 20 x 30 meter area. At R's signal the group in possession of the ball attacks the regular goals defended by a support player and the other group. If the support player gains possession he plays the other group into the attack.

Duration
10/12 attacking moves, 1 every 2 minutes.

Variations
1) The support player plays with the group that attacks.
2) Attacking move playing two-touch soccer.
3) 5 against 3 in area **1** and 2 support players in area **2**.

Objectives
Rapid solutions for counter-attacks.

Exercise n. 236

Players
12 + 2 support players
+ 1 goalkeeper.

Description
Groups 4A and 4B assisted by two support players play in area **1**. At R's signal the support player plays the ball for two of the players from group A on the break. One of these players starts from the wing, the other from the goal-line. They attack the regular goal defended by the goalkeeper and two of the players from group B. The two players from group B start from the other side of the pitch and from the goal-line.

Duration
8/10 counter-attacks, 1 every 2 minutes.

Objectives
Technical and tactical perfection of moves in counter-attack.

Variations
1) First time passes or two-touch soccer in area **1**.
2) Two players from each group start from outside the playing area to alternate with their teammates in area **1**.
3) A sweeper in front of the goalkeeper.

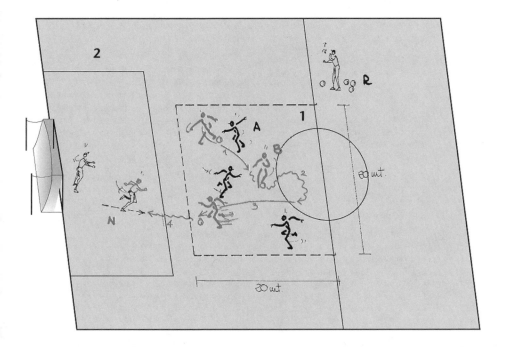

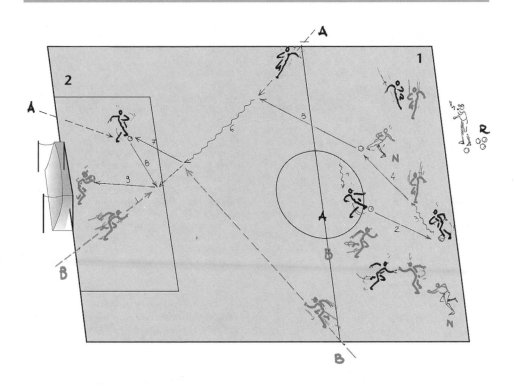

Exercise n. 237

Players
12 + 1 goalkeeper.

Duration
8/10 attacking moves, 1 move every 2 minutes.

Objectives
Tactical move for effective openings on the break.

Description
Groups 4A and 3B play two-touch soccer in a 30 x 30 meter area. When group 3B gains possession it passes the ball to a teammate outside the quadrangle. This teammate plays the ball on over the halfway line to another two teammates of the same group. These two players must attack the regular goals in under 30 seconds. The goal is defended by a goalkeeper and by two players who come into play once the player from outside the area plays the long pass.

Variations
1) 2 attack and 4 defend.
2) A sweeper inside the area and 3 attacking players.
3) 3 attacking players and 2 defenders, all players play three-touch soccer.

Exercise n. 238

Players
10 + 1 goalkeeper.

Duration
7/8 attacking moves, 1 every 2 minutes.

Objectives
Tactical move for effective moves on the break.

Description
Groups 4A and 3B play three-touch soccer in a 20 x 40 meter area **1**. When group 3B gains possession it plays the ball to its teammate in the central corridor. They all move forward in attack while group A defends. The goal is defended by a goalkeeper and another defender who comes into play from off the goal-line once the player in the central corridor receives the ball. The player in the corridor plays the ball back to his teammates who are moving forward with him.

Variations
1) A single player moves out to receive the pass from the corridor and hits a first time shot at goal.
2) 5 attack, 4 defend with a sweeper in the middle of the area.
3) 4 defend 5 attack with headers to finish.

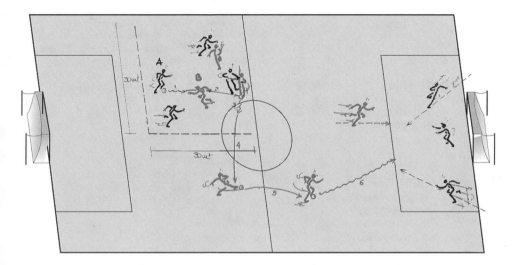

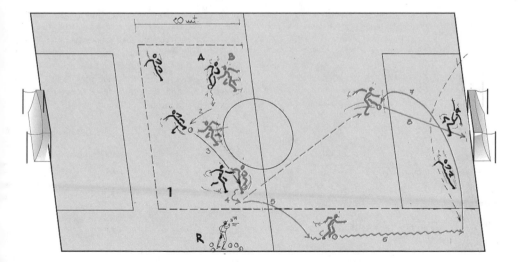

Exercise n. 239

Players
12 + 1 goalkeeper.

Duration
8/10 counter-attacks.
1 every 2 minutes for
each group.

Objectives
1) Specific move for per-
fection of players in
attack.
2) R's signal speeds up
the movement of group
A from area **1**.

Description
Groups 6A and 4B play three-touch soccer in
area **1**. At R's signal group 6A attacks the goal
in area **2** which is defended by group 4B and
two players who come into play when the
attacking players move into area **2**. Group 6A
must shoot from outside the box in under 30
seconds.

Variations
1) 6 against 3 in area **1** + 1 support player.
2) Invert the positions of the players.
3) Group A attacks from the wings moving out
of area **1**.

Exercise n. 240

Players
10 + 2 support players
+ 1 goalkeeper.

Duration
10 counter-attacks,
1 every 2 minutes.

Description
Groups 5A and 5B play each other for possession and are assisted by the two support players who dribble the ball. At R's signal the
group in possession attacks the regular goal
defended by the goalkeeper and the other
group. The two support players play long
passes. If the attacking team loses possession
the roles are inverted.

Objectives
Tactical organizations
for new solutions and
structuring of attacking
and defensive moves.

Variations
1) 5 against 5 with a sweeper in front of the
goalkeeper.
2) At R's signal another two players come onto
the field for the attacking move.

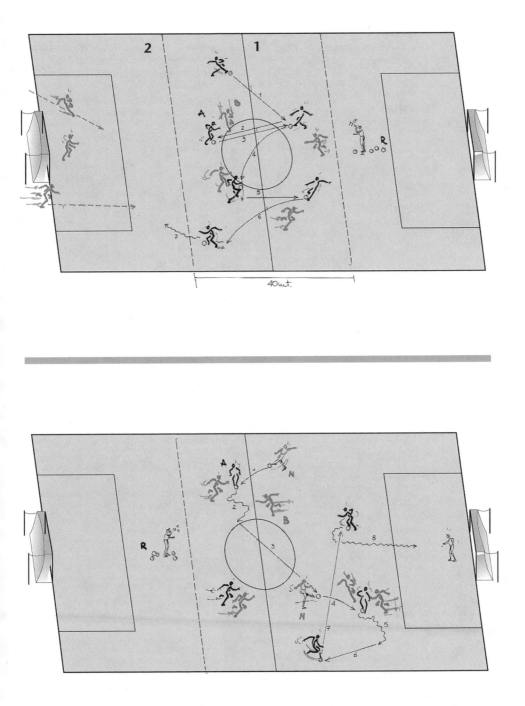

Exercise n. 241

Players
13 + 2 support players
+ 2 goalkeeper.

Duration
Five 7 minute sessions.

Objectives
Tactical build-up to improve moves on the break.

Description
Groups 3A and 3B play three-touch soccer in area **1** to shoot at the regular goals and the small ones on the side of the field. Group 4C plays three-touch soccer against group 3D which plays without any restrictions in area **2**. Group C defends the regular goals and attacks the small goals on the sides of the pitch while group D attacks the regular goals and defends the small goals. At R's signal the teams exchange balls with a long pass and the group that gains possession attacks the regular goals in the opposite area on the break.

Variations
1) The support player assists with 1-2 combinations.
2) The goalkeeper joins in the counter-attack.
3) The small goals are placed on the goal-line.

Exercise n. 242

Players
12 + 1 support player
+ 1 goalkeeper.

Duration
20 minutes. R alternates the play in the two fields every three minutes.

Objectives
Fast solutions for the counter-attack.

Description
Groups 6A and 6B play three-touch football in area **1** to shoot on the small goals. At R's signal the team in possession of the ball attacks the small goal in area **2** while the other group defends. A support player moves in to play as a defender from the halfway line.

Variations
1) Increase the small goals in area **2**.
2) One group plays first time passes and the other has no restrictions.

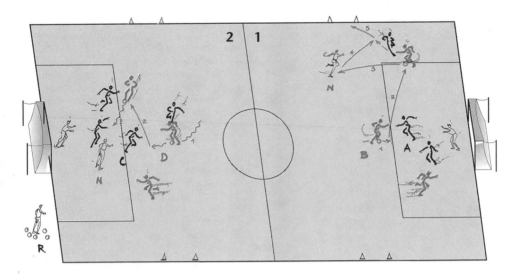

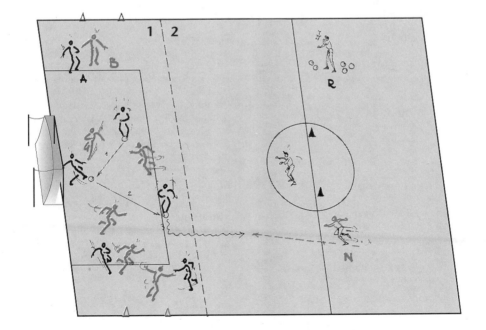

Exercise n. 243

Players
16 + 2 goalkeepers.

Duration
Counter-attack every
2 minutes.

Objectives
Perfection of technique
in counter-attack.

Description
Groups 6A and 6B play each other to attack the
five meter goals on the sides of the field in area
1. Before the shot a player must dribble the ball
across a 3 meter space. At R's signal the team
with the ball moves into area **2** and attacks the
three small goals while the other team defends.
Two players move onto the pitch to act as
defenders with the team that lost possession.

Variations
1) The counter-attack is followed by a long
pass from the team with the ball without R
giving any signal
2) A support player plays in area **2**.
3) The group on the break plays three-touch
soccer.

Exercise n. 244

Players
10 + 2 support players
+ 2 goalkeepers.

Duration
Five or six minute
sessions.

Objectives
A specific attacking
technique is required
from group A in area **1**
and a defending tech-
nique in area **2**.

Description
Groups 5A attacks the goal defended by group
5B in area **1**. When group B gains possession it
passes it to a support player who puts a player
from area **2** on a run with a long pass down
the wing. This player passes the ball to a teammate for the finishing shot without moving
outside the area indicated by the dotted lines.
The two support players play on the sides of
area **1**.

Variations
1) The support players with group A playing
in attack can shoot from the wings.
2) 7 against 7 and the attacking players finish
with headers.

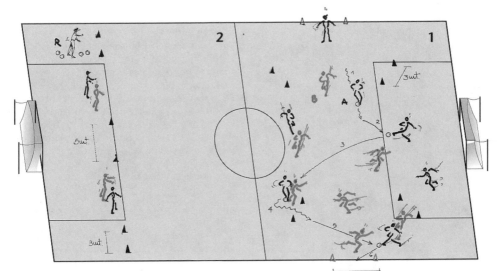

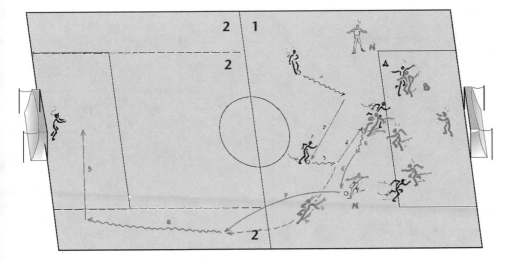

Exercise n. 245

Players
14 + 1 support player
+ 2 goalkeepers.

Duration
Six 5 minute sessions.

Objectives
Tactical move that concentrates on the mobility of the attack.

Description
Groups 5A and 5B play each other on a reduced forty meter area. At R's signal the group in possession, which would be A in this case, attacks the opponents' goal on the break. Only two players attack while one player from group B follows them. Two players come into play from off the goal-line to defend. The players left, 3A and 4B, attack on the break from R's quick pass from the edge of the field. 4B attack and 3A defend assisted by two other defenders who come into play from off the goal-line.

Variations
1) The attacking players play three-touch soccer during the counter-attack.
2) At R's signal the entire group attacks and only three players from the other group defend.

Exercise n. 246

Players
18 + 1 support player
+ 1 goalkeeper.

Duration
Five 6 minute sessions.

Objectives
Adaptation of players to the tactical orientation in defense and in attack.

Description
A regular pitch is divided into three areas. Groups 9A and 9B play each other for possession. They are both limited to three touches. In each area three players play each other for each group. The play moves from the defender to the midfield player to the attacking player through areas **1**, **2** and **3**. If the opponent gains possession he must respect the direction of the move. The support player must assist 1-2 combinations and shots at goal.

Variations
1) At R's signal the direction of the play is switched.
2) The support player can move into the attacking area with the ball.

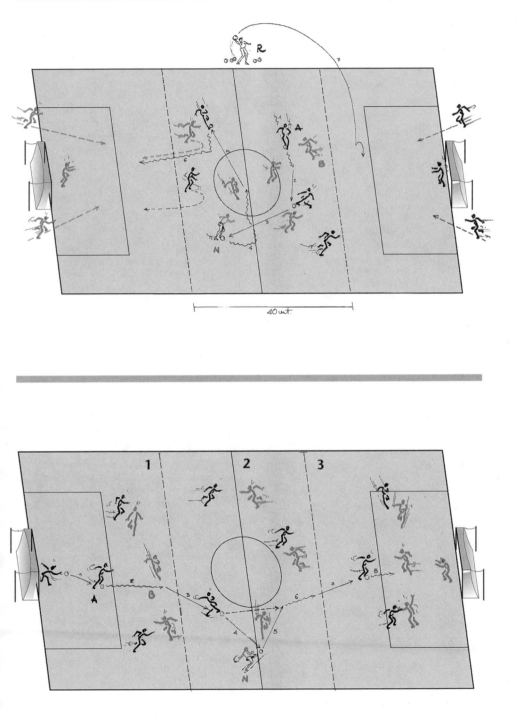

Exercise n. 247

Players
12 + 2 support players + 1 goalkeeper.

Duration
Five 5 minute sessions.

Description
Groups 4A and 4B play with a support player to keep possession in area **1**. At R's signal the ball is passed to area **2** for the finish. Group 2A plays group 2B with a support player. Whoever is in possession of the ball must play a 1-2 before the shot. Two players from area **1** can move into area **2** to assist the play (one in attack, the other in defense).

Objectives
1) Fast build-up in area **1** and finish in area **2**.
2) The two support players assist with rapid passes and 1-2 combinations.

Variations
1) 3 against 3 in area **1** with 2 support players.
2) 5 against 5 in area **1** and 2 against 2 in area **2**.

Exercise n. 248

Players
11.

Duration
Eight 3 minute sessions.

Description
Group 4B plays to maintain possession while attacked by group 7A. When group A wins possession one of its players must dribble the ball across the small area followed by one of the players from group B.

Variations
1) Limit touches of the ball.
2) Play with two support players.
3) Attack the small area from the wings only.

Objectives
Defense through constant pressure from the opponent.

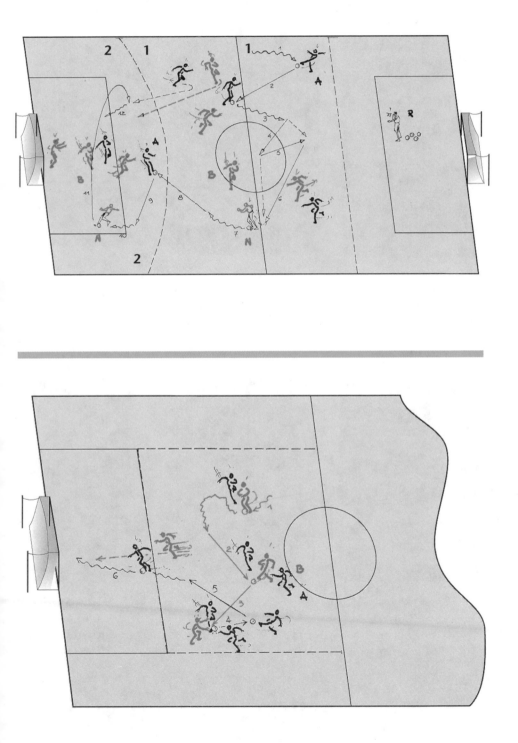

Coaching Books from REEDSWAIN

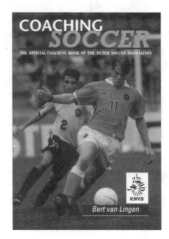

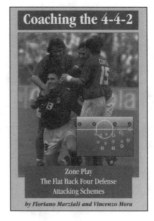

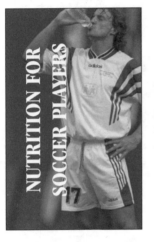

Coaching Books from REEDSWAIN

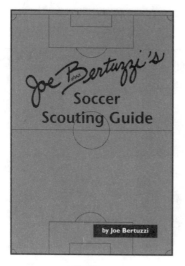
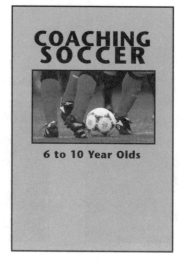

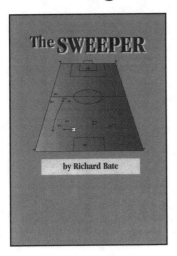

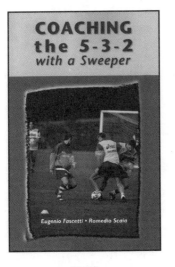
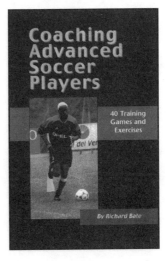

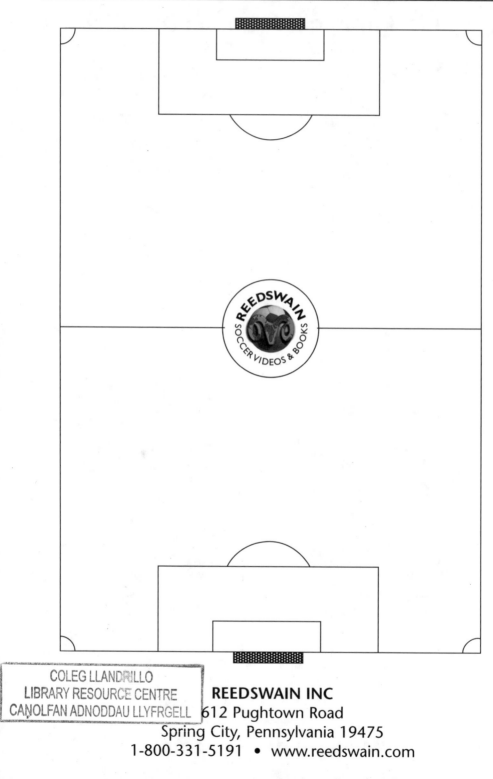

REEDSWAIN INC
612 Pughtown Road
Spring City, Pennsylvania 19475
1-800-331-5191 • www.reedswain.com